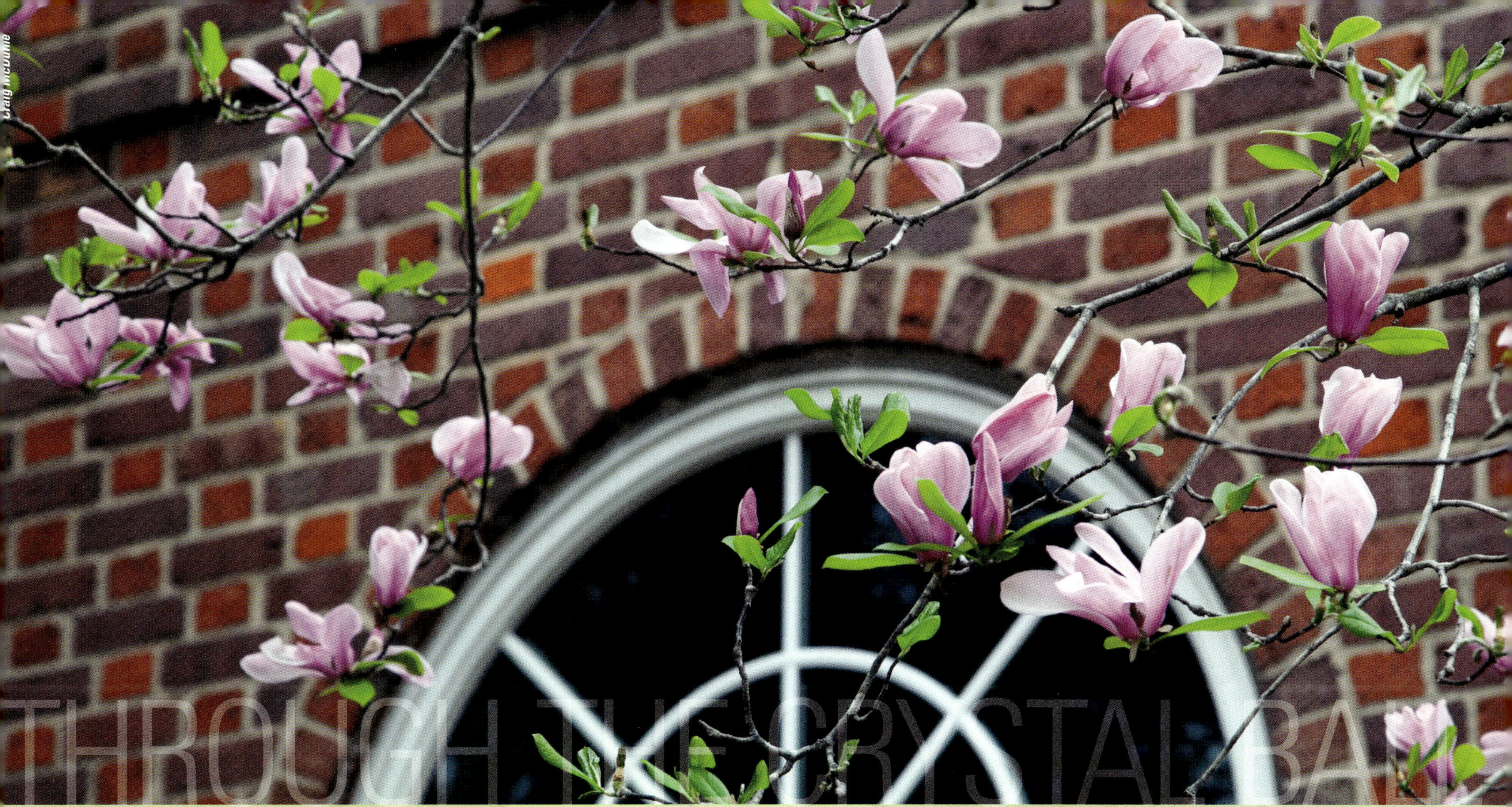

THROUGH THE CRYSTAL BALL

Through the Crystal Ball of the Chancellor's Residence

North Carolina State University • 1928–2012

MARGARET RUTH LITTLE

NCSU Libraries • Raleigh, North Carolina • 2013

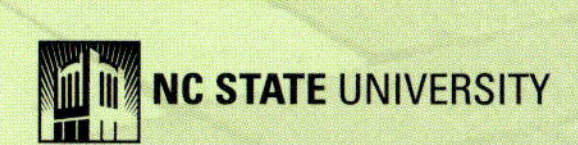

Craig McDuffie

Published in the United States by the NCSU Libraries.

Printed in the United States of America
NCSU Libraries • 2 Broughton Drive • Raleigh, NC 27695-7111 • www.lib.ncsu.edu
Printed by Four Color Print Group • Designed by Linda Noble
Front cover photo by Roger Manley • End paper and back jacket photos by Craig McDuffie

ISBN: 978-0-615-85972-9

Contents

PREFACE

Just as the glass globe on the newel of the staircase near the front door reflects a panoramic view of the rooms, the furniture, and the world outside, the house too is a crystal ball through which we can view NC State University's history through most of the twentieth century.

Through the Crystal Ball of the Chancellor's Residence: Preface

In November 1927 President Eugene Brooks and his wife Ida were preparing to move into their new home, the final element of the 1920s modern building campaign of the State College campus. The *Alumni News* marveled at the transformation of the site and the speedy construction of the house. "The president's new home, just across Hillsboro Street, opposite College Court Pharmacy, is rapidly nearing completion, and the grounds are receiving a generous portion of shrubbery and sod. Even full-sized trees have found themselves torn out of their old places and transplanted into more symmetrical positions. The home itself is of red brick construction, modern but dignified in its twin chimney effect at each end, with its deep-green blinds, and with its unpretentious entrance."[1]

The campus had evolved over the previous forty years as a collection of Victorian and Classical Revival buildings built sporadically on random sites. Initially crowded into a single building—Holladay Hall—at its founding in 1887, the college's classrooms and laboratories of each curriculum became more specialized with each new building. Yet even in the 1910s some of the scientific departments shared space in single buildings, the library occupied part of a multi-purpose building, and the president lived off campus. Not until the early 1920s did State College commission a plan for its future growth. Between 1921 and 1928 architect Hobart Upjohn and landscape architect Warren Manning created a master plan that rationalized the campus into zones of activity arranged around open courtyards. The team transformed the campus into a modern academic village with paved roads and walkways, landscaped open spaces, and new classroom buildings, dormitories, a large rotunda-lit library, and a grand gymnasium. An official presidential residence was the culmination of the modernization of the 1920s, a statement to the citizens of North Carolina that State College had become a modern professional institution. Just across Pullen Road from the original campus buildings, the new residence symbolized a new day for the college.

President Brooks, who had presided over most of the new construction, was the first president to enjoy an official residence. He and his wife Ida worked hard with architect Upjohn to perfect the house's layout, giving special attention to the kitchen service areas, to servants' quarters,

ABOVE: President and Mrs. E.C. Brooks, circa 1930. Courtesy of Luzette Callum Brown.

FACING PAGE: Glass globe on the newel post of the Chancellor's Residence staircase. Photograph by Craig McDuffie, 2012.

ABOVE: Fountain, rear garden of the Chancellor's Residence, installed during the Harrelson years. Photograph by Craig McDuffie, 2012.

and to the dining room and living room to insure that they were large enough and well equipped to handle the needs of entertaining. The residence was designed with dual facades to meet its public and private purposes, Janus-like with its public front face to the world and its private rear face towards the woods of Pullen Park. As President Brooks and his family moved into their new home in 1928, they looked optimistically toward State College's future.

Through the Crystal Ball of the Chancellor's Residence, North Carolina State University, 1928–2012, brings you inside the original Chancellor's Residence at 1803 Hillsborough Street to share the vision and the family life of each of the university's leaders, from President Brooks to Chancellor Woodson, the last executive who resided there. This is not the fantastical journey of Alice in Wonderland, but a tribute to the remarkable men and women whose service made NC State University into one of the premier institutions of higher education in the country. We also celebrate the architectural character of the residence and its place in the orderly modern redesign of the entire campus.

Just as the glass globe on the newel of the staircase near the front door reflects a panoramic view of the rooms, the furniture, and the world outside, the house too is a crystal ball through which we can view NC State University's history through most of the twentieth century. We look back at the Roaring Twenties, the Depression, three wars, the Civil Rights and women's rights struggles of the Sixties, and the expansion across Western Boulevard to the Centennial Campus. Ten remarkable leaders have steered the university into the future while living in the residence. Ten first ladies and one first gentleman have presided over events at the residence and projected familial and university hospitality to the public. The joys and challenges of eighty-four of the university's 125 years are mirrored in the Chancellor's Residence.

The idea for this book was born in late 2011 as Chancellor Randy Woodson and his wife

Susan were moving from the residence to "The Point," the new residence on Main Campus Drive at Centennial Campus. The stately Georgian Revival house had projected the dignified image of the leaders of the institution since its completion in 1928, and Susan wanted to celebrate the role of the old house during its eighty-three years.

The stories, photographs, and history are based on research in the NCSU Libraries Special Collections Research Center and on interviews with many individuals: the present chancellor and his family, the five previous chancellors and their families, correspondence and interviews with the families of the leaders who are no longer with us, and interviews with the staff who have worked at the residence.

Each member of the project team contributed his or her special talents. Susan Nutter, vice provost and director of the NCSU Libraries, Gregory Raschke, associate director for collections and scholarly communication at the NCSU Libraries, and Eli Brown, head of the Special Collections Research Center, coordinated the publication project. Todd Kosmerick, University Archivist, and Jennifer Baker, University Library Technician, cheerfully retrieved obscure records and created digital scans of worthy photographs. Catherine Bishir, curator of architecture special collections at the Libraries, provided creative inspiration, biographical information on architects who worked on campus, and reviewed successive drafts. Murray Downs, emeritus professor of history at NCSU, reviewed the manuscript for historical accuracy. Linda J. Noble provided the fresh, engaging graphic design; Craig McDuffie contributed the richly-detailed photographs of the former residence. The work of photographers Roger Winstead, Matthew Robbins, Edward T. Funkhouser, Roger Manley and others also enhances the book. Thanks to the good memory of Banks Talley, longtime dean of students and later vice-chancellor, a number of individuals in these pages were able to be contacted.

The joyful spirit of this house book derives from the chancellors and their families who shared their memories and entrusted their photographs and scrapbooks to me. Many thanks to Luzette Brown and Sally Kelly, granddaughters of President Brooks; Alice Steele and Andy Caldwell, children of Chancellor Caldwell; Marly Thomas, wife of Chancellor Thomas; Chancellor Larry Monteith and his wife Nancy; Chancellor Bruce Poulton; Chancellor Marye Ann Fox; Chancellor James Oblinger; and Chancellor Randy Woodson and his wife Susan. Former housekeepers Doris Atwell and Bobbie Cross shared their stories of how the residence entertained its many guests.

Names of the college and of its chief executive have changed due to growth and administrative evolution over the past 125 years. Established in 1887 as the North Carolina College of Agriculture and Mechanic Arts, its name changed to the NC State College of Agriculture and Engineering in 1917 and to NC State University in 1965. The text will use the institution's popular names for each era: A & M College, State College, and finally NC State University. The college head was known as the president until the title changed to vice-president in 1931, then to dean of administration. Since 1945 the chancellor has led the institution. The University of North Carolina at Chapel Hill, the mother of higher education in the state, will be referred to as UNC-Chapel Hill.

Gaze into the crystal ball for a quick look backward in time to the beginning of the college in the late 1880s and its slow and steady growth until the 1920s.

Note

1 "Many Changes Occurring around the Campus of N.C. State College," *Alumni News (North Carolina State College)*, November 1927, pages 4–5.

THE BACKSTORY

"No white marble pillars support the building whose cornerstone we have laid here today.... In its walls are nothing but North Carolina brick and her still more solid sandstone. It is a goodly and worthy structure."

CHAPTER ONE

The Backstory: North Carolina College of Agriculture and Mechanic Arts: 1887 to the 1910s

The deepest layer in the crystal ball on the newel post of the President's Residence reveals the heady years of the 1880s, when the promise of higher education for industrial and agricultural workers in North Carolina was finally fulfilled by the establishment of North Carolina's first land-grant college. Since 1862 when the national Morrill Land-Grant Act granted annual funds to North Carolina to endow a college to teach agriculture and mechanic arts for the "liberal and practical education of the industrial classes," the state's share had gone to the University of North Carolina at Chapel Hill. The university's classical atmosphere was not compatible with practical education and a separate college became necessary. Two forces in Raleigh spurred the creation of the new college for industrial and agricultural education. Leonidas LaFayette Polk, the state's first commissioner of agriculture, had organized a statewide farmers' movement and promoted a new land-grant college in the 1870s through his journal, *The Progressive Farmer.* In 1884 the Watauga Club, an association of young, progressive capitalists led by Walter Hines Page, editor of the *State Chronicle*, a Raleigh newspaper, was formed to promote an industrial school in Raleigh.[1]

In 1887 the State Legislature authorized the new college. The bill established the college on sixty-two acres one mile west of town donated by Raleigh capitalist Richard Stanhope Pullen, and specified that the directors of the State Penitentiary would provide bricks and convict labor for the new college's buildings.[2] A precise drawing by David Clark, an 1895 alumnus and first president of the North Carolina Textile Association, depicts the fledgling campus ten years later. He showed Main Building (Holladay Hall) at the lower right; Watauga Hall in the center; First, Second, Third, and Fourth dormitories with porches at left; and Primrose Hall at the top right. All buildings face east toward Raleigh.

ABOVE. Bird's eye view of A & M College, 1897. Drawing by David Clark. NCSU Libraries Special Collections Research Center.

FACING PAGE. The first class of students to attend NC State stands on the steps of Holladay Hall in 1889. NCSU Libraries Special Collections Research Center.

LEFT: The first freshman class posing in front of and inside the college's main building, Holladay Hall, in 1890. President Holladay and the faculty stand near the porte-cochere. Charles L. Carson, a Baltimore architect, designed the building. NCSU Libraries Special Collections Research Center.

RIGHT: Primrose Hall, completed 1896. Photograph by Edward T. Funkhouser, 2003. NCSU Libraries Special Collections Research Center.

Main Building contained all the college facilities, including offices, classrooms, and dormitory rooms, with a kitchen, dining hall, gymnasium and laboratories in the basement. Its architectural character derives from simple bold massing, broad arched openings, and fine brick and stonework rather than from expensive materials and ornate decoration, as befits the mission of a college established to promote the practical education of the industrial classes.[3] At the laying of the cornerstone on August 22, 1888, speaker William J. Peele lauded it as a North Carolina temple without columns. "No white marble pillars support the building whose cornerstone we have laid here today.... In its walls are nothing but North Carolina brick and her still more solid sandstone. It is a goodly and worthy structure."[4]

Alexander Quarles Holladay (1839–1909), the first president of the college from 1889–1899 and an alumnus of the University of Virginia and the University of Berlin, had served as lieutenant under General Braxton Bragg during the Civil War. Holladay taught history, and the other four original professors taught agriculture, horticulture, chemistry, mathematics, practical mechanics, English, and bookkeeping. The first freshman class numbered seventy-two students. The very first student, Walter Mathews, lived until 1967.[5]

Primrose Hall, built in 1896 for the horticulture department, has a tower that is a landmark along Hillsborough Street. Its arched doors and arched and circular windows continue the popular Romanesque Revival style of Holladay Hall. It is named for William Stuart Primrose (1848–1909), a founding member of the Watauga Club and longtime chairman of the college's Board of Trustees. Greenhouses extended from the south and west sides during the era when it was used for horticulture classes and laboratories.

A & M College entered the twentieth century with a new president, George T. Winston, who served from 1899–1908. Three hundred students were enrolled in 1899, and by the end of his tenure there were 446. President Winston, a Latin professor, graduated from UNC-Chapel Hill and served as its president (1891–1896), and then as the first president of the University of Texas (1896–1899). Under his leadership the college stretched out along Hillsborough Street with

Pullen Park

ABOVE: A view of Pullen Park, a pastoral retreat for college students, from the 1909 issue of the Agromeck *yearbook (page 152). NCSU Libraries Special Collections Research Center.*

Pullen Park, donated to the city by Raleigh industrialist Richard Stanhope Pullen at the same time as his donation of the site for State College, was the first public park in North Carolina. Pullen and his park keeper, Wiley A. Howell, planted the old "red and rocky cow pasture" with magnolias, cedars, and willow oaks and shrubbery in 1888. They built bridges over the railroad track and Rocky Branch, a circular pavilion, and a circular concrete fountain. State College students played baseball at the park's Red Diamond field across Pullen Road from the dormitories and enjoyed the beauty of the Cedar Walk and the Cedar Circle, both apparently planted by Pullen. Pullen Hall, named for the college's benefactor, with an imposing columned front portico, was completed in 1902 just south of Primrose Hall. Its main floor contained an 800-seat auditorium, its second floor housed the college library, and its basement a dining hall. The building served as a center of campus life until its destruction by arson in 1965.

"Pullen Park History," City of Raleigh website, http://www.raleighnc.gov/arts/content/PRecRecreation/Articles/PullenParkHistory.html; Murray Scott Downs and Burton F. Beers, *NC State University: A Pictorial History* (Raleigh: NC State University Alumni Association, 1986), 23.

LEFT: Tompkins Hall, completed 1901. 1901 photograph. NCSU Libraries Special Collections Research Center.

RIGHT: Watauga Hall, completed 1903. Charles W. Barrett and Frank K. Thomson, architects. Photographic Postcard. NCSU Libraries Special Collections Research Center.

separate buildings for its pre-eminent disciplines of agriculture (Patterson) and engineering (Winston).

Daniel A. Tompkins, one of the South's leading textile mill architects and promoters, established the new textile program and constructed this textile school, where students learned to operate and repair the latest weaving machinery, along Hillsborough Street in 1901. Tompkins had designed and built textile mills throughout the Piedmont of North Carolina, especially in his adopted city of Charlotte. The building incorporated the latest innovations in fireproof construction, ventilation, and natural lighting—wrapped in a fashionable skin of Romanesque Revival brickwork and arched windows. A five-story turreted tower announced the twentieth century spirit of machine power that would be spread throughout the state by the young men studying in this building. The building burned in 1914 but was rebuilt the same year. Its tower was lowered to two stories in a later, less romantic, era.[6]

The new Watauga Hall, a dormitory replacement for the 1893 dormitory that had burned, is a three-story brick edifice with quoined corners and a wide arched entrance similar to those designed by H.H. Richardson, a Boston architect who created his own version of the Romanesque Revival style. Watauga Hall's designer, Charles W. Barrett (1869–1947), moved to Raleigh in 1899 and was one of the city's most prolific architects until his departure in 1910.[7]

The placement of the agriculture building on the campus was so important that the college enlisted the opinion of landscape architect Frederick Law Olmsted Jr. of Boston, son of famed landscape architect Frederick Law Olmsted Sr., to select the site. Olmsted visited the campus in 1904 and chose a spot on Hillsborough Street opposite Horne Street, the entrance to the State Fairgrounds, the yearly exposition of agricultural products. Agricultural Hall was renamed Patterson Hall for Samuel Ledgerwood Patterson (1850–1908), state commissioner of agriculture in the 1890s, who believed that the building belonged in downtown Raleigh rather than on a college campus. The building has housed the Agriculture Department (now the College of Agriculture and Life Sciences) since it was built. Prolific Charlotte architect C.C. Hook and his partner Frank M. Sawyer designed the imposing Classical Revival building of buff brick with a rusticated granite basement podium and a pedimented triple-arched entrance with Corinthian pilasters.[8]

Engineering received its own equally imposing and stylish building in 1910, named for second

LEFT: Agricultural Hall (later Patterson Hall), completed 1905. C.C. Hook and Frank M. Sawyer, architects. NCSU Libraries Special Collections Research Center.

RIGHT: Patterson Hall, detail. This detail illustrates the robust Classical Revival pilastered wings of buff and orange brick, with arched windows, created by architects Hook and Sawyer. Photograph by Edward T. Funkhouser, 2002. NCSU Libraries Special Collections Research Center.

LEFT: The 1911 Building, completed 1909. 1930 photograph. Harry P.S. Keller, architect. NCSU Libraries Special Collections Research Center.

RIGHT: Winston Hall, completed 1910. Frank B. Simpson, architect. Photograph by Edward T. Funkhouser. NCSU Libraries Special Collections Research Center.

president George T. Winston. It was designed by Frank B. Simpson (1883–1966), a Raleigh native who studied in 1897–1898 at State College in the "sub-freshman class" that provided technical education to young men unable to enroll as freshmen. Simpson worked outside the state and returned to Raleigh by 1907. The building's central arched entrance is sheltered by a monumental pedimented portico supported by clusters of brick columns with Ionic capitals. The red brick walls contrast boldly with the prominent gray brick columns and pilasters and white window trim, conveying the strong color and texture contrasts beloved by early twentieth-century architects.[9]

Daniel Harvey Hill Jr., an English professor who was one of the college's original faculty members, served as president from 1908 to 1916. Student enrollment grew to 723 during these years, and the Agricultural Extension Service, an outreach program that took the latest advances in farming to every county in the state, was established.[10]

The dormitory, completed in 1909 and named in honor of the Class of 1911, which pledged to end the unpopular tradition of freshman hazing by upperclassmen, is said to have been the largest dormitory in the South at the time.[11] Architect Harry P.S. Keller (1869–1938) of Maryland established his own practice in Raleigh in 1907.[12] The exuberant red brick dormitory has been called a "robust and free"

version of the classical style. Windows with large red and white arches and free-floating white plaques set into the brick animate the façade above the sedately columned porch stretching across the central two-story section. Its profusion of white keystones recall the Moorish arches in medieval mosques of southern Spain.

At Leazar Hall, built in 1912 as the dining hall, architect Keller settled into a more sedate Colonial Revival style, recalling the harmonious form of Thomas Jefferson's home, Monticello. Tall arched windows with keystoned fanlights illuminate the original dining hall. It is named for Augustus Leazar (1843–1905), who assisted Charles Dabney in drawing up a bill to establish the college while serving in the state House of Representatives in 1885. While this bill failed, a second attempt was successful in 1887. The debating society, Leazar Literary Society, met here; the rival Pullen Literary Society met in Pullen Hall. These societies disappeared when student government was established in the 1920s.[13]

By the 1910s Raleigh's streetcar suburbs had grown out to the State College campus, aided by the trolley line along Hillsborough Street that terminated at Patterson Hall, facing Horne Street, the entrance to the State Fair. In this photograph *(above, right)* a youth group from the North Carolina State College campus boards a chartered trolley on Hillsborough Street for an excursion around Raleigh during the summer of 1917.

LEFT: Leazar Hall, completed 1912. Harry P.S. Keller, architect. Photograph by Edward T. Funkhouser, 2005. NCSU Libraries Special Collections Research Center.

RIGHT: Hillsborough Street (Raleigh), 1917. NCSU Libraries Special Collections Research Center.

Notes

1 David A. Lockmiller, *History of the North Carolina State College of Agriculture and Engineering of the University of North Carolina, 1889–1939* (Raleigh: The General Alumni Association of the North Carolina State College of Agriculture and Engineering, 1939), 22–8; Murray Scott Downs, "Historical Sketch of NC State University," Historical State website, http://historicalstate.lib.ncsu.edu/histories/historical-sketch-of-north-carolina-state-university.

2 "History," *N.C.S. College of Agriculture and Engineering, Directory of Faculty and Students, 1930–1931* (Raleigh: The College, 1930), 1:302. R.S. Pullen (1822–1895), a patron saint of higher education in the 1870s and 1880s, had acquired the defunct Peace Institute and put it into the hands of the Presbyterians in 1872 "in order to preserve it as a seminary for the education of young women." Pullen and Greensboro developer R.T. Gray donated the original ten acres for the Normal and Industrial School in Greensboro (now the University of North Carolina at Greensboro); Lockmiller, 35–6.

3 William B. Bushong, "Charles L. Carson," in *North Carolina Architects & Builders: A Biographical Dictionary* (Raleigh: NCSU Libraries Digital Scholarship & Publishing Center, 2009–), http://ncarchitects.lib.ncsu.edu. The state Executive Mansion designed by Philadelphia architect Samuel Sloan, under construction at the same time, was also built of penitentiary brick.

4 Ibid.

5 Downs, "Historical Sketch of NC State University"; Marguerite E. Schumann, *Strolling at State: A Walking Guide to NC State University* (Raleigh: NC State University Alumni Association and NC State University Foundation, 1973), iv, 1–2.

6 Catherine W. Bishir and Michael T. Southern, *A Guide to the Historic Architecture of Piedmont North Carolina* (Chapel Hill: University of North Carolina Press, 2003), 127, 503–4; Schumann, 34.

7 William B. Bushong, Dave Delcambre, and Catherine W. Bishir, "Charles W. Barrett," in *North Carolina Architects & Builders*. Barrett often worked in partnership with architect Frank K. Thomson in an office on Fayetteville Street. Barrett's uncle, George F. Barber, headquartered in Knoxville, Tennessee, was famous as the most prolific mail order architect in the United States in the early 1900s. In addition to Watauga Hall, Barrett and Thomson's work in Raleigh included the monumental Municipal Building and Auditorium of 1910 (destroyed) and a substantial bank.

8 Lockmiller, 74; Downs and Beers, 24; Michelle Michael, "C.C. Hook," in *North Carolina Architects & Builders*.

9 Felicity Smith and Catherine W. Bishir, "Frank B. Simpson," in *North Carolina Architects & Builders*.

10 Downs, "Historical Sketch of NC State University."

11 Schumann, 32.

12 William B. Bushong, Dave Delcambre, and Catherine W. Bishir, "H.P.S. Keller," in *North Carolina Architects & Builders*. Keller remained in Raleigh until at least 1930, but his work during the 1920s has not been identified. During the Depression he worked as a superintendent of school construction for eastern North Carolina.

13 Downs and Beers, 30.

RIGHT: The balusters of the President's Residence staircase curve around the upper landing. Photograph by Craig McDuffie, 2012.

A MODERN CAMPUS

...the college set out to create a rational and orderly campus with well-defined sectors to accommodate its changing vision and growing needs.

CHAPTER TWO

The Roaring Twenties: Creating A Modern Campus for State College

The crystal ball of the Chancellor's Residence most clearly reflects the Twenties, the decade of its construction. From 1921 to 1928 the State College campus was completely transformed according to a master plan created by architect Hobart Upjohn and landscape architect Warren Manning. The master plan put into physical form the new vision and reorganization of the college developed during the presidency of Wallace C. Riddick from 1916 to 1923. Its realization under President Riddick and his successor, Eugene Brooks, produced a campus suited to a growing, modern, professional institution.

President Riddick's transformative term of office had begun during the momentous era of World War I, when the campus became the site of intensive military training. Near the end of the war in 1917, to reflect the increasing emphasis on professional education and pure science, the college name had dropped the term "mechanic arts" and became the North Carolina State College of Agriculture and Engineering. The student body had risen from 732 in 1914 to nearly 1000 in 1920. In 1922 the college commissioned U.S. Bureau of Education specialist George Zook to develop an intensive reorganization plan for State College. Implemented in 1923, the recommendations contained in the Zook Report separated the college into three professional schools: engineering, agriculture, and science and business, each headed by a dean.[1]

Simultaneously, the college set out to create a rational and orderly campus with well-defined sectors to accommodate its changing vision and growing needs. As stated in the *Alumni News* in 1924, a campus plan was sorely needed: "Many of the first buildings were put up with scant consideration of the probable growth of the College. As a consequence the older part of the campus exhibits a patchwork effect, with the buildings bearing little relation to each other or to the general landscape plan as a whole. This rather unsightly arrangement of buildings, and the overcrowding of the original campus was due, in large measure, to the amazing growth of the College."[2] Because of the "amazing growth" and as part of a statewide investment in its public colleges and universities, funding for new construction came from the state General

ABOVE: Holladay Hall, rear entrance, State College shield with monogram. Hobart Upjohn, architect (1928). Photograph by Roger Winstead, 2003.

FACING PAGE: The Vermont marble entrance portico of Brooks Hall, built in 1925 as the D.H. Hill Library, Hobart Upjohn, architect. Photograph by Roger Winstead, 2003.

ABOVE: Master Plan, ca. 1924. The first phase of the Memorial Tower built in 1920–1921 at the corner of Pullen Road and Hillsborough Street in honor of the college's fallen students in World War I is not shown, nor is the President's Residence, built in 1928 and the last of the new construction of the 1920s. Hobart Upjohn, architect, and Warren H. Manning, landscape architect. Private owner; image courtesy of Matthew Robbins.

Assembly, which appropriated $600,000 for the 1921–1923 biennium and more than doubled that sum to $1,350,000 for the 1923–1925 biennium.[3]

The college had employed national educational expert Zook to create a modern, professional college organization, and it selected a nationally known architect, Hobart Upjohn of New York, and a landscape designer, Warren Manning of Massachusetts, to develop and execute a master plan. Upjohn and Manning began their work at State College in about 1921 to execute improvements funded by the first legislative authorization. Upjohn designed the Gold and Welch Dorms, constructed in 1921, and Manning was employed as landscape architect for the college sometime prior to 1923.

In 1923, with the larger state appropriation in mind, the college leadership embarked on a more ambitious project to include five new buildings and additions to three others. In April 1923 the college Building Committee—composed of Samuel F. Patterson (chair), O. Max Gardner, T.T. Thorne, P.S. Boyd, and ex-officio member President W.C. Riddick—interviewed five architectural firms for the project. Upjohn was unanimously selected for the contract. In order to determine locations for the new buildings, he invited Warren Manning back to the college to collaborate on a ten-year master campus plan.[4]

The two men released a preliminary report on the new campus plan in the spring of 1923. In June 1923 Manning presented and explained the plan to the State College Building Committee, composed of Samuel F. Patterson; R.N. Page; the new college president, Eugene Brooks; former President Riddick; and state senator Mark Squires.[5] Within a year the plan was approved, adopted, and was published in the May 1924 *Alumni News*. The cover featured Upjohn and Manning's powerful image of the plan, a birdseye view of the campus signed by the pair. The accompanying article explaining the proposed changes was appropriately entitled, "Future Growth of State College To Be Along Orderly Lines."

Upjohn and Manning's challenge, to remake the campus by inserting new buildings among existing buildings while creating an "orderly" format for growth, was more complex than the campus expansions taking place concurrently at the University of North Carolina at Chapel Hill and at Duke University in Durham, which developed open sites. The State College team accomplished its campus plan with little demolition, making wise use of the scarce state appropriations of the 1920s. The two men also made skillful use of the Beaux-Arts principles of design in which both had been trained to create a clearly organized campus of well-defined zones and spaces unified by a shared architectural vocabulary.

Throughout the nation, planners and landscape architects in the early twentieth century worked in a mode known as the "City Beautiful" movement, based on the urban planning precepts of the *École des Beaux-Arts* in Paris. Like the planners of the grand city centers of Europe in the nineteenth century, American planners sought to beautify and organize the city by separating it into zones of usage, connected by boulevards linking grand vistas of monumental classically-styled buildings, with traffic controlled by roundabouts and plentiful parks and open spaces. American landscape architect Frederick Law Olmsted helped to design the Chicago World Columbian Exposition of 1893, which popularized the City Beautiful movement and Beaux-Arts architecture in the United States. One of Olmsted's chief assistants was his employee Warren Manning.[6]

Popular in the United States from the late nineteenth century through most of the first half of the twentieth century, the Beaux-Arts tradition of design—whether for individual buildings, estates, college campuses, or entire cities—arranged spaces according to well-defined hierarchies and relationships among the component parts. Painting and sculpture were often integrated into the architectural ensemble. The predominant architectural style was Beaux Arts classicism, with its monumental porticos and ornate stone cornices that defined many public buildings in the United States, but in some cases architects employed "colonial" and Gothic Revival themes.

The parallels between the campus expansions at the University of North Carolina at Chapel Hill and at State College in the early twentieth century are striking: both institutions commissioned master plans along Beaux-Arts principles and employed New York City architects to design the new buildings. At Chapel Hill after World War I, as at State College, one thousand students were crowded into the dorms and classrooms. The university drew up a master plan for growth in 1913, reworked it in 1919, and hired the prestigious New York City architectural firm of McKim, Mead and White in 1919 to design classrooms, dormitories, a library, a gymnasium and other structures. Most of the buildings were constructed in a Colonial Revival theme of red brick and white trim—requested by the university as a return to the simple "colonial" style of the university's first buildings—that gave coherence to the campus, including the new quadrangle that extended south of the old South Building to the Beaux-Arts classical Wilson Library.[7]

Upjohn and Manning were well equipped to apply these principles to the transformation of State College. Both were experienced in the Beaux-Arts design tradition, while Manning was also skilled in creating less formal, naturalistic landscapes and complexes. Both were also practical men accustomed to working with local clients, budgets, and situations.

Hobart Upjohn (1876–1949), the architect for both the master plan and the 1920s building campaign, was a New Yorker and the scion of a famous family of New York–based architects. His grandfather, Richard Upjohn, an English architect who immigrated to the United States, helped to introduce the Gothic Revival style into the country. He designed a major church in the style in 1846—Trinity Church on Wall Street in New York City and in the late 1840s designed Christ Church in downtown Raleigh, one of the first and finest Gothic Revival churches in North Carolina. Richard's son Richard M. Upjohn designed many churches, as well as the Connecticut State Capitol.

Upjohn was trained as a mechanical engineer but opened his own architectural office in New York City in 1905 and designed around 150 churches, hospitals, schools, and houses, nearly one-third located in North Carolina. Like his fellow architects, Upjohn's knowledge of European architectural styles and Beaux-Arts principles allowed him to tailor a style to suit a building's function. He maintained an office in Grand Central Terminal, New York City, and a staff of two architects, Aaron G. Alexander and Otto F. Langman.

Hobart received numerous commissions in the state through wealthy North Carolinians familiar with his grandfather's work, designing nearly fifty church and educational buildings between 1908 and ca. 1930, including some of his finest work in the country—among them churches in Burlington, Wilmington, Roanoke Rapids, Chapel Hill, and a chapel and parish house for Christ Church in Raleigh. Hobart Upjohn likely received the State College commission through his Raleigh connection to Christ Church and through his previous work in the textile mill town of Roanoke Rapids, including a small church and an imposing and modern high school, for industrialist Samuel F. Patterson, a member of the State College Board of Trustees in the early 1920s.[8]

Many of State College's earlier buildings had been the work of local and in-state architects, a tradition for the land-grant institution to stimulate the state's economy. When Upjohn was hired, a series of anonymous postcards sent to the Raleigh *News and Observer* spewed spleen at the hiring of an out-of-state firm. Columnist Nell

Battle Lewis published an editorial asserting that Upjohn's architectural proficiency was needed, because "we certainly know of no one in North Carolina who can equal. As evidence of his remarkable talent, one has only to point to the Presbyterian Church in Chapel Hill and the parish house of Christ Church in Raleigh. ... which constitute two of the most conspicuous architectural ornaments in North Carolina."[9]

Landscape architect Warren H. Manning (1860–1938) designed parks, estates, city plans, college campuses, subdivisions and more during his long career from the 1890s to the 1930s. Manning's professional roots were nurtured at his father's nursery and during eight years working under Frederick Law Olmsted, whose genius had shaped many of the great developments of the late nineteenth century, including Central Park in New York City and urban plans for Milwaukee, Buffalo, and Washington, D.C. Manning worked under Olmsted on many of these projects, adding the skills of land use planning to his expertise with plants. In 1896 he left Olmsted's office to practice on his own in Boston and later Billerica, Massachusetts. His horticulture background led him to create a naturalistic design aesthetic with native plant materials that reflected the unique character of the American landscape, in contrast to the prevailing formal approach of the Beaux-Arts and City Beautiful movements. State College was one of many beneficiaries of Manning's gentle approach to shaping existing conditions and native plants into what he called his "wild gardens."[10] His largest contribution to the expansion of the State College campus was the creation of a functional infrastructure consisting of a modern network of roads and walkways for vehicular and pedestrian traffic and the linkage of the new campus across the railroad tracks to the existing campus. The design of new roads as well as reworking of old roads, sidewalks, curbs and gutters, and planting and grading were all necessary improvements.[11]

LEFT: Hobart Upjohn, architect for North Carolina State College during the 1920s. Photograph courtesy of Avery Architectural and Fine Arts Library, Columbia University.

RIGHT: Warren Henry Manning, landscape architect for North Carolina State College during the 1920s. Photograph, ca. 1925, courtesy of Stan Hywet Hall & Gardens, www.stanhywet.org.

The plan that Upjohn and Manning presented in 1923 and which was published in 1924 was the first master plan for the campus, the State College of the future. Their aerial view of 1924 depicted their vision. It showed where buildings would be placed to augment the groupings of buildings already in existence. The view showed

LEFT: Gold Dormitory, completed 1921. ca. 1967 photograph. Hobart Upjohn, architect. NCSU Libraries Special Collections Research Center.

RIGHT: Page Hall, completed 1922. The Mechanical Engineering Building is named for Walter Hines Page (1855–1918), a member of the Watauga Club and supporter of the establishment of NC State University. Page served as editor of the State Chronicle and as ambassador to Great Britain from 1913–1918. Hobart Upjohn, architect. Photograph by J.D. Paulson. NCSU Libraries Special Collections Research Center.

an engineering court bounded by the existing Tompkins Hall (the textile building) and Winston Hall (the engineering building) along the edge of a large valley and at the west edge by the existing 1911 dormitory. To the west, an agricultural grouping was achieved by retaining Patterson Hall (the agriculture building) and creating a large courtyard to its rear defined by seven new buildings: Broughton Hall at the south end, Polk Hall and two additional buildings along the west side, and Ricks, Withers, and Daniels Halls along the east side. A new building for the School of Science and Business and the Graduate School was planned behind Holladay Hall.

An extensive student life zone was developed on the south and east sides of the existing campus. Several existing buildings in the student group included dormitories, Leazar dining hall, a student center (the YMCA), and Riddick Field on the east side of the campus. To expand this group, a new library was to be located on Pullen Road in place of the old First, Second, and Third Dorms, beside the new Gold and Welch dormitories. Syme Dormitory would be enlarged and a new bridge would be built across the railroad tracks to the south to provide a link to a new dormitory court and a new gymnasium and athletic field. Riddick Field would be rebuilt as Riddick Stadium.

The redesigned campus would receive a new infrastructure of roads, paths, a sewer and drainage system, and a heating and power plant. Manning redesigned the area around Holladay Hall through a skillful treatment of original landscape features and by laying out new drives. As shown on the master plan, a new main entrance on Hillsborough Street just west of the existing Memorial Tower connected with Cedar Drive and another new drive ran east-west along the north side of Riddick Field. The valley in front of 1911 Dormitory would be terraced and provided with steps. Two bridges and an underpass would connect the newly-opened south campus, south of the railroad tracks, with the old campus.[12]

As the Upjohn-Manning team began their campus transformation, leadership passed in 1923 from President Riddick to Eugene Clyde Brooks, who would see their great work through. "We cannot properly understand people until we know the sources of their joys," declared the new president in his inaugural address.[13] Architecture was clearly one of President Brooks's joys, and he worked closely with Upjohn to guide the modernization and expansion of the campus already begun by President Riddick. Brooks had a close ally in Clarence Poe, editor of *The Progressive Farmer,* who became a member of the Building Committee by 1923 and chairman of the Board of Trustees by 1928.

To implement the master plan, Upjohn designed a harmonious ensemble of eleven Classical Revival buildings in red brick, arranged in traditional quadrangles that not only accommodated the growth but endowed the campus with a professional stature and echoed the designs of early English university quadrangles and distinguished colleges throughout America.[14] Built as funding became available, these buildings include Gold Dormitory, 1921; Welch Dormitory, 1921; Page Hall, 1922; Syme Dormitory (center and south wing), 1924; Bagwell Dormitory, 1925; Frank Thompson Gymnasium, 1925; D.H. Hill Library, 1925; Daniels Hall (physics and electrical engineering), 1926; Polk Hall (animal husbandry), 1926; and the President's Residence, 1928. A vehicular bridge, Pullen Bridge, was built across the tracks in 1925 to allow access to the new Bagwell Dormitory and Thompson Gymnasium.[15] Of the fourteen new buildings on the master plan, Upjohn designed nine of them, which

BELOW: View of Daniels Hall (physics and electrical engineering), 1926, Hobart Upjohn, architect. Ca. 1950 photograph. NCSU Libraries Special Collections Research Center.

LEFT: Thompson Gymnasium (now Theater), completed 1925. Hobart Upjohn, architect. Photograph by Edward T. Funkhouser, 2009. NCSU Libraries Special Collections Research Center.

RIGHT: Bagwell Dormitory, completed 1925. Hobart Upjohn, architect. NCSU Libraries Special Collections Research Center.

were built from 1921–1928. Some of the 1920s buildings were designed by other architects who followed the master plan and whose plans were reviewed by Upjohn. Thomas W. Cooper and G. Murray Nelson of Raleigh designed Ricks Hall, built in 1922 for the Agricultural Extension program. Ross Shumaker, head of the architecture department within the Civil Engineering curriculum, designed Peele Hall for liberal arts in 1928 to fit within Upjohn's scheme.[16]

In addition to designing new buildings, Upjohn renovated and designed additions to a number of older buildings, including doubling the size of Leazar Hall, the dining building, about 1923 and working on Patterson Hall in 1924. His culminating renovation was for Holladay Hall in 1928–1929, where he reworked the interior for administrative offices and installed a new rear entrance pavilion of brownstone. Above the rear entrance he included a brownstone shield with State College's monogram, probably to emphasize the importance of this elevation, which faced most of the campus buildings. The monogram had probably been created after the college changed its name to the North Carolina State College of Agriculture and Engineering in 1917.

Throughout the project, Upjohn had a close working relationship with President Brooks and the college's Board of Trustees, visiting the college a number of times and keeping in close contact through letters. His assistant, A.G. Alexander, sometimes made site visits and often corresponded with college officials on behalf of Upjohn. During the summer of 1924, when he had been at work on State College for several years, Upjohn took a two-month study and rest tour to Italy, leaving his business in the hands of Alexander, who traveled from New York to Raleigh to report to the college Building Committee.[17] In the next few years, perhaps inspired by the Renaissance buildings of Italy, Upjohn created some of the finest buildings of his career. These included churches such as the Village Chapel of 1925 in Pinehurst, North Carolina, an unusually elegant version of St. Martin in the Fields (an early eighteenth century classical church in London by James Gibbs), and the First Presbyterian Church of 1927 in Concord, North Carolina, with elegant proportions, inventive arcades enclosing an exterior courtyard, and a distinctively-lit interior. During the decade he also designed Colonial Revival style buildings in a Moravian-inspired mode for the growing campus at Salem College in Winston-Salem.[18]

In 1927, towards the end of his campus tenure, Upjohn assisted in creating the Department of Architectural Engineering. He gave two lectures to the engineering students in fall 1927 exhorting them to create new distinctive styles expressive of the current era and declaring that construction materials determined style. Upjohn taught a class on the art of building in the new department the following year. The new department head, architect Ross Shumaker, urged the creation of a separate school of architecture, but this did not happen until 1948.[19]

Manning installed his infrastructure and landscaping at the campus at least through the end of 1925. Twenty thousand dollars were spent from 1921 to 1923 alone on sewer lines, drainage, and curbed and guttered roadways. One of his first tasks was to realize the master plan's vision for the campus's largest and most beautiful open space, described as "that broad sweep of the campus lying between Holladay Hall and the 1911 dormitory and the territory adjacent thereto."[20] The area was graded, new drives and walks installed, and shrubbery and trees were planted. Under Manning's supervision, students in the Civil Engineering curriculum at the college performed some of the work for course credit and were paid for other portions of the work. Engineering student W.T. Cox became the supervisor of landscape construction in 1924.[21] Work continued on the remainder of the campus for a number of years, especially the development of the new south campus beyond the railroad tracks. Creating pedestrian walkways was a constant priority, and by late 1927 there was a "continuous ribbon of concrete from the entrance at the post office, by the dining hall, and to the south end of 1911 … and another walk extending from Pullen Hall to the railroad bridge at the end of Sixth (Welch) Dormitory."[22]

During the 1920s, Upjohn's suave classicism and Manning's rational urban planning had tamed the haphazard pre-World War I campus into a harmonious whole. Upjohn's conscious turn toward a restrained and scholarly neoclassical architecture contrasted dramatically with the college's existing industrial and free classical aesthetic. Upjohn modulated his classicism into a softer Colonial Revival mode for dormitories and into a grander Neoclassical Revival vocabulary with commanding stone entrance pavilions for educational buildings. The red brick, white wooden trim, and chaste entrances of Gold and Welch dormitories of 1921 harmonize with Bagwell Dormitory of 1925, which exhibits a quiet Colonial Revival design with its massive long front and rear elevations enlivened by pilastered pediments enclosing arched windows. By contrast, Page Hall, built in 1922 for the Mechanical Engineering department, is a large-windowed Neoclassical-style building with a dignified entrance frontispiece with stone Doric pilasters supporting a robust entablature carved with the building's name. A special challenge because of its size and multiple purposes was Polk Hall, the animal husbandry building of

LEFT: Polk Hall (animal husbandry), completed 1926. Hobart Upjohn, architect. NCSU Libraries Special Collections Research Center.

RIGHT: Polk Hall, detail showing relief sculpture. In classical architecture the ox skull motif, dating to the sacrificing of ancient oxen, was commonly used. Here it emblemizes the building's function of animal husbandry. Photograph by Edward T. Funkhouser, 2007. NCSU Libraries Special Collections Research Center.

1926, which combined the livestock industry and the dairy industry educational facilities in one four-story building, the largest building erected on campus to that date. It contained a complex variety of spaces for the dairy and animal industries, including classrooms, a library, a large second-floor auditorium, a judging pavilion similar to a show ring, a slaughter room, a meat-cutting room in the north livestock industry section, laboratories for milk and cheese, an ice cream manufactory, a refrigerating plant, a sterilizing room, and extension and research quarters.[23] Upjohn broke up its mass with a pair of sections defined as classical entrance pavilions—stone frontispieces with Corinthian pilasters, pediments, and balustrades above the roof cornice—and relief carving of a steer skull in a classical motif suitable to the purpose of the building.

Upjohn's most costly buildings were the Frank Thompson Gymnasium and the D.H. Hill Library of 1925. The gymnasium reflects the simple large volumes of an ancient Roman bath, with a Palladian entrance porch at the front and the effect of an arcade along each side wall, which lights the space inside with immense windows. Hill Library, the college's first library that had its own building, is Upjohn's campus masterpiece. A prime example of the Beaux-Arts aesthetic, the red brick and white marble building has a pedimented marble entrance

portico, large windows, a roof balustrade, and a domed rotunda. The portico columns of Vermont marble feature Tower of the Winds capitals. The octagonal entrance hall with inlaid marble floor rises to a high dome, with walls of cream stone and an Italian marble balustrade around the balcony. The large reading room across the rear half of the building has five glass skylights and tall arched windows that repeat a format employed in many neoclassical-inspired libraries. President Brooks saw the importance of its architectural character. He believed that the library would not only give the college the reading resources it needed, but would have the "silent influence of its beauty and dignity on the lives of the students who frequent its halls. There will be no need for signs that 'Quiet must be observed,' for to enter the rotunda of the building, with its high arched dome, its exquisite blending of colored marbles, its soft light, is to feel something of the hush that makes one instinctively whisper in the Library of Congress."[24]

This building, Upjohn's masterpiece, served as the campus library until the new D.H. Hill Library was built in 1953. After the library moved, the building became Brooks Hall, the home of the School of Design (now College of Design) to the present. Brooks Hall is named for Eugene Clyde Brooks (1871–1947), who led the college from 1923 until 1934.

LEFT: D.H. Hill Library (later Brooks Hall), completed 1925. 1936 photograph. Hobart Upjohn, architect. NCSU Libraries Special Collections Research Center.

RIGHT: Brooks Hall, detail of a "Tower of the Winds" capital of the marble portico. Hobart Upjohn, architect. Photograph by Edward T. Funkhouser, 2001. NCSU Libraries Special Collections Research Center.

constructed in the 1830s, the columns in the House of Representatives chamber have Tower of the Winds capitals. Early twentieth-century architects favored this simplified Corinthian capital in their classical buildings.

ABOVE: View of campus, 1938. Photograph by U.S. Army Air Corps. NCSU Libraries Special Collections Research Center.

The capitals, a chaste version of the Greek Corinthian order, substitute a row of palm leaves for the usual upper row of acanthus leaves. The order was taken from a first or second-century B.C. tower in Athens and was published in eighteenth-century antiquities books that influenced the Greek Revival in England and America.[25] At the North Carolina State Capitol,

With the library completed, the Upjohn and Manning team had transformed State College into a modern campus ready for its twentieth century destiny. The last building of the great campaign—not shown on the master plan—would be the President's Residence, which Upjohn designed in collaboration with its first occupants, President Brooks and his wife, Ida, as a proper home for the head of the growing college. As the November 1927 *Alumni News* noted proudly, "everything about the college is in a process of growth and change."[26]

The end result of the 1920s campus expansion, with Hobart Upjohn's buildings and Warren Manning's landscape design, appears in this 1938 aerial view of campus. At center right is the engineering court around the Court of North Carolina and at upper right is the agriculture court consisting of Patterson, Ricks, and Polk Halls. The Chancellor's Residence is at lower left; Thompson Gymnasium, at upper left. The Memorial Bell Tower, completed in 1937, stands near the campus entrance. Over the next several years various things, such as the Carillon, were installed into the Bell Tower.

Notes

1 Anonymous report, Office of the Chancellor Records, UA002.001.001, box 3, NCSU Libraries Special Collections Research Center; Downs, "Historical Sketch of NC State University."

2 "Future Growth of State College to Be Along Orderly Lines," *Alumni News (North Carolina State College)*, May 1924, 2.

3 State College of Agriculture and Engineering Request for Permanent Improvement 1927–1929, Office of the Chancellor Records, UA002.001.001, box 3, folder 1.

4 Minutes of the Building Committee, Board of Trustees, 16 April 1923, Office of the Chancellor Records, UA002.001.001, box 1, folder 7. The other architects interviewed were Cooper and Nelson, Wilson and Berryman, G. H. Wells, and James A. Salter.

5 Minutes of the Building Committee, Board of Trustees, 29 June 1923, Office of the Chancellor Records, UA002.001.001, box 1, folder 10.

6 "Warren H. Manning," *Wikipedia*, accessed January 14, 2013, http://en.wikipedia.org/wiki/Warren_H._Manning.

7 M. Ruth Little, *The Town and Gown Architecture of Chapel Hill, North Carolina, 1795–1975* (Chapel Hill, N.C.: The Preservation Society of Chapel Hill, 2006), 51–4.

8 Gerald Allen, "Hobart Upjohn," in *North Carolina Architects & Builders*; Hobart Upjohn, letter to Samuel F. Patterson, 6 June 1923, Office of the Chancellor Records, UA002.001.001, box 1, folder 7. The Christ Church chapel and parish house were completed in 1914. Upjohn designed the All Saints Episcopal Church in Roanoke Rapids in 1917. Samuel F. Patterson, a Roanoke Rapids industrialist, Episcopalian, and a nephew of Samuel L. Patterson, for whom Patterson Hall at State College is named, hired Upjohn to design the state-of-the-art Roanoke Rapids Junior-Senior High School in 1920, which Patterson constructed at his own expense.

9 Nell Battle Lewis, "Incidentally," *Raleigh News and Observer*, September 2, 1923, Office of the Chancellor Records, UA002.001.001, box 1, folder 10.

10 Biography of Warren Henry Manning, Stan Hywet Hall and Gardens website, http://www.stanhywet.org/images/company_assets/512F1C7F-0D64-4A5E-9D91-785DC064755F/c6ca1_Warren_Henry_Manning.pdf; "Warren H. Manning," *Wikipedia*, accessed October 25, 2012. While working at State College in 1924, Manning was hired by trustee Clarence Poe to create a plan for his new subdivision, Longview Gardens, along New Bern Avenue in east Raleigh. The development was laid out in the late 1930s according to plans by a different landscape architect. M. Ruth Little, "Longview Gardens Historic District," National Register Nomination (Raleigh: N. C. Historic Preservation Office, 2009).

11 *Alumni News (North Carolina State College)*, February 1923, 1.

12 "Future Growth of State College to Be Along Orderly Lines."

13 Eugene Clyde Brooks, "The Relation of Education to Public Welfare" (Inaugural Address), May 26, 1924, Office of the Chancellor Records, UA002.001.001, box 1, folder 17.

14 Cynthia de Miranda, "Historic Architectural Resources Survey Report, TIP No. U-4447," Hillsborough Street Improvement Project #1 (Raleigh: N. C. Historic Preservation Office, 2004), 3.

15 Berry and Becton dorms completing the court were constructed with WPA funds in the 1930s.

16 Request for payment from college budget officer A. S. Brower to State of North Carolina, July 22, 1927, Office of the Chancellor Records, UA002.001.001, box 3.

17 Letters, Office of the Chancellor Records, UA002.001.001, box 1.

18 Allen, "Hobart Upjohn."

19 "Architect Says Profession Art," *Raleigh News and Observer*, October 13, 1927; "Hobart Upjohn Will Join State College Faculty," *Raleigh News and Observer*, May 15, 1927; Downs and Beers, 73.

20 "What the College Wants from the General Assembly," *Alumni News (North Carolina State College)*, February 1923, 1; "W. T. Cox to Work Out New Landscape Scheme," *Alumni News (North Carolina State College)*, January 1924, 3. In the later twentieth century the space became known as the Court of North Carolina because it was rumored to contain one hundred trees, one for every county in the state. The area never had that many trees, and Hurricane Fran destroyed a number of them in 1996.

21 *Alumni News (North Carolina State College)*, January 1924, 3, and October 1924, 5.

22 "Many Changes Occurring Around The Campus of N.C. State College," *Alumni News (North Carolina State College)*, November 1927, 5.

23 "The New Animal Husbandry Building," *Alumni News (North Carolina State College)*, October 1925, 2.

24 Susan Iden, "New Library Masterpiece of Architecture," *Raleigh Times*, reprinted in *Alumni News (North Carolina State College)*, October 1925, 1–2.

25 Bannister Fletcher, *A History of Architecture on the Comparative Method*, 16th ed. (New York: Charles Scribner's Sons, 1956); Catherine Bishir, interview by the author, January 10, 2013.

26 *Alumni News (North Carolina State College)*, November 1927, 5.

MODERN BUT DIGNIFIED

As State College's size and reputation grew, so too did the need for an elegant setting for special occasions, such as graduation receptions, welcome events for alumni, and the entertainment of special guests.

CHAPTER THREE

A "Modern But Dignified" Home for the President

Ever since Alexander Holladay became the first president of the North Carolina College of Agriculture & Mechanic Arts in 1887, the college's leaders had lived in rented houses across Hillsboro Road (present Hillsborough Street) from the campus. Holladay lived across the street between Enterprise Street and Maiden Lane, and most of the college's professors lived on Maiden Lane, the first planned neighborhood in what was then called West Raleigh, intended to house college faculty and their families. By about 1906 Raleigh's streetcar system made this neighborhood accessible to downtown. Daniel Harvey Hill Jr., the third president, led the college from his home at 2 Maiden Lane. It is said that the steps on the north side of the present Memorial Tower were built to ease Hill's walk from his home to Holladay Hall in his later years. President Wallace Carl Riddick and his family lived in a Queen Anne-style house of the 1890s on Hillsboro Road near the present large traffic roundabout. [1] Thus a presidential home on the campus may have seemed a dispensable facility for the 1920s campus expansion.

In contrast to State College, the University of North Carolina at Chapel Hill had built its first president's house about 1793, beginning with a frame house that is now lost. The third and current president's house at 402 East Franklin

FACING PAGE: President's Residence, front entrance portico supported by wooden columns with Tower of the Winds capitals. Photograph by Craig McDuffie, 2012.

BELOW: Hillsborough Street as seen from NC State campus, early 1900s. Note the original Pullen Baptist Church sanctuary at the far right. The street appears in a military battalion photograph (catalogue number 0000278). NCSU Libraries Special Collections Research Center.

ABOVE: President Carl Riddick's house. Photograph from the Agromeck, *1918, page 30. NCSU Libraries Special Collections Research Center "Historical State" website.*

Street is a frame "Southern Colonial"-style house built in 1907, with a welcoming monumental portico and one-story side porches that evoke an antebellum plantation house. The style was favored for wealthy Southerners at the turn of the twentieth century and asserted the New South's link with the plantation aristocracy of the antebellum South. William Friday lived here as president of the university system from 1956 to 1986 and hosted many gatherings of faculty, staff, and students, as have subsequent presidents.[2]

As State College's size and reputation grew, so too did the need for an elegant setting for special occasions, such as graduation receptions, welcome events for alumni, and the entertainment of special guests. In 1923, acknowledging the need for an official residence for the president and a venue for college ceremonies and events, State College trustees authorized an architect identified only as Nelson (presumably G. Murray Nelson, who designed Ricks Hall) to do a tentative plan for a president's home with a budget of $40,000.[3] Actual construction of the residence, however, was deferred to the end of the building campaign of classrooms, dormitories, library, gymnasium, heating and power plant and other facilities that would occupy most of the 1920s. Relegating the residence to the end of the 1920s construction kept faith with the college's land grant ideal—to leverage its state building funds for maximum effect to provide higher education for practical purposes.

After his campus design work was largely complete, campus architect Hobart Upjohn was given a strict budget of $30,000 to produce a suitable abode. In order to stay within budget, Upjohn determined at the beginning of the design process that the house could not exceed 6,900 square feet. He made this calculation by dividing the $30,000 budget by an estimated construction price per cubic foot of $.40, which allowed an interior volume of 71,496 cubic feet for the cost of $28,598.[4]

The site chosen, a spacious three acres on Hillsborough Street not far from previous presidents' residences, lay near the intersection of Pullen Road, one of the campus entrances. Pullen Memorial Baptist Church stood on the east side, at the corner of Cox Avenue, and the College Court Pharmacy anchored the Oberlin Road corner across the street. Holladay Hall, the administrative building, sat across Pullen Road from the site. To the rear stretched the picturesque woods of Pullen Park. This position placed the president's residence at the junction of town and gown, community and college.

President Brooks and his wife Ida were intensely interested in the design of their new home and exacted as attractive and practical a house within

LEFT: President's Residence front elevation, ca. 1929. The car in the driveway is probably the Brooks family car. Mrs. Brooks did the driving, since President Brooks never learned how. Courtesy of Luzette Callum Brown.

RIGHT: President's Residence, ca. 1930. State Archives of North Carolina. Albert Barden, photographer.

the budget as possible. Mrs. Brooks had firm ideas on its function as the college's space for hosting receptions for faculty, staff, students, and distinguished guests. She consulted Upjohn in person on April 21, 1927, and, as the architect noted, made the following requests: "the dining room to be at least seventeen feet square and the living room seventeen by thirty feet in size. The kitchen is to be eleven by fourteen with a pantry with a breakfast alcove at the end with a table and fixed benches on either side. There is to be side terraces and a rear porch."[5]

In July 1927 Upjohn presented to President and Mrs. Brooks his plans for a gracious brick residence that continued the 1920s classical themes of the library and classroom buildings but in a simpler Colonial mode. In these plans, Flemish bond brick walls rise into a roof parapet with twin chimneys at each end and two-story wings. Large windows with operable louvered shutters provide plentiful light. A semicircular portico with paired columns with Tower of the Winds capitals, like those used at the library, shelters the central entrance facing north to Hillsborough Street. Above it, a casement window opens to a balcony. The main block contains a central hall with staircase, living room to the west, a study, dining room, and kitchen to the east. The stairs rise to a central hall, with two bedrooms and one bathroom along the front and two bedrooms and one bathroom along the rear. A hallway leads to the bedroom and bath in the east wing, accessible by a secondary stair from the kitchen. The west side wing contains an arcaded porch with a sleeping porch with casement windows upstairs, adjoining the master bedroom in the west rear corner of the main block. As originally planned, the east service wing contained the kitchen, a garage in the basement, a basement stair, and a stair to an upstairs bedroom and bath.

Ida Brooks next met with Upjohn on May 31, and she requested a servant's quarter and a change in the front entrance. She wanted a maid's bedroom and bath in the basement beneath the kitchen in place of the garage on his original plan. Mrs. Brooks's changes to the plan were wise and traditional. Her suggestion acknowledged that the servant's bedroom would be an indispensable component of the functioning of the official residence and in keeping with regional usage.

Mrs. Brooks also objected to the location of the staircase in the front hall as crowding the front entrance. She asked the architect to change the Hillsborough Street entrance so that it did not enter under the main staircase. Upjohn recalled that he "persuaded her that the best circulation would be obtained this way."[6] He wished to preserve a full vista to Pullen Park at the rear, for if the stair had been located in the south end of the large central hall, it would have blocked the view of the park.

Like the Roman God Janus with two faces, one facing forward, the other to the rear, the President's Residence fulfilled dual purposes: a public façade to the town, a private façade for the president and his family toward the garden. A belief repeated by several families who lived in the house is that it had originally faced to the south, away from Hillsborough Street. This presumption is logical because the south entrance—a glazed door with wide sidelights and fanlight—is wider than the front door and because the driveway extends to the south. But the architect labeled the north side of the house as the front from earliest correspondence, and stipulated a south (rear) porch with steps leading down. This porch was eliminated during the design phase because its cost came in over budget.

Upjohn was following a long-established tradition of country houses with closed facades to the front and open, light-filled spaces to the rear. There is ancient precedent for dual facades—many country estates presented a closed public facade and an open face to the rear, the private realm that overlooked a pleasant natural vista. Aristocratic mansions from Governor Tryon's colonial palace in New Bern, North Carolina, to Washington's Mount Vernon had closed facades and open rear elevations overlooking water views. In the same vein, suburban residences and country estates built by elite families along the east coast in the early twentieth century often featured a floor plan in which the front entrance opened beneath the stair into a hall with large windows and doors overlooking a rear garden. The colonial revival-style Norman Stockton House in Winston-Salem, designed in 1929 by Philadelphia architect Charles Barton Keen, has such a plan. Across the rear is a suite of rooms looking out to a terraced garden.[7]

In early July Mrs. Brooks sent the architect a list of her requirements for the service wing, which led him to change its whole arrangement. Upjohn's July 5, 1927, letter to Dr. Brooks assured him that he had altered the plans to suit her. "You will note that there is a Breakfast Room off the Study, which is the same arrangement that I have put in the Rankin House in Fayetteville. This gives a larger kitchen, a good sized pantry, an entry, outside entrance to the kitchen, with a cold closet and single bedroom and bath for the service above, which can be used as a Master's Bedroom and bath, also, in the basement underneath, would be one servant's bedroom and bath for the negro help."[8]

The Rankin House in Fayetteville, designed by Upjohn about 1927, is a large Colonial Revival-style two-story brick residence with a two-story service wing.[9]

The following blueprints *(pages 38–42)* are the final version of the house design, after budget considerations caused the omission of the rear porch and one terrace, and a maid's room was substituted for the basement garage. The bedroom and bath above the kitchen could function either as a servant's quarter or as a child's bedroom.

President Brooks wrote to Upjohn on September 2 requesting a few more changes to the plans: adding fireplaces in upstairs bedrooms 1 and 4 and cutting a door between bedrooms 2 and 4. The exterior wood cornices concerned the president because the original plans had called for marble. Brooks asked if the cornices could be fabricated of terra cotta or cast stone to make them more permanent. Upjohn added a fireplace in bedroom 1 and a door in bedroom 2, but explained that a fireplace could not be added in bedroom 4 because it was so small that it would cramp the placement of a bed.[10] The wood cornices remained in order to stay within budget.

The Jewel-Riddle Company of Sanford, contractors, began construction in September 1927 and laid approximately 180,000 bricks to support and enclose the 6,900-square-foot residence. The major subcontractors were Will J. Carter, electrical wiring; Dermont Plumbing Company, plumbing; and Carolina Heating and Engineering Company, heating. Brick was apparently supplied by the Cherokee Brick Company. By November the house was nearly complete.[11]

ABOVE: President's Residence, early 1930s. Courtesy of Luzette Callum Brown.

LEFT President's Residence, view of the rear, ca. 1928. State Archives of North Carolina. Albert Barden, photographer.

RIGHT: President's Residence, rear view, 1929. NCSU Libraries Special Collections Research Center.

Among the final expenditures for the house were rugs, window shades, and the purchase of a Kelvinator from Carolina Power and Light Company for $210 instead of the cold closet shown in Upjohn's plan. Mrs. Brooks must have been pleased to have an electric refrigerator instead of an ice box that needed daily ice deliveries. The total cost of the house construction was $28,740.16, and the architect's fee of $1,257.67 left a balance of $2.17 from the $30,000 legislative appropriation. Upjohn's careful control of the costs of design and construction was a tribute to his experience and professionalism.

The November 1927 *Alumni News* reported that the three-acre site required extensive landscaping to deal with its uneven terrain. The grounds were improved with topsoil and shrubbery in late 1927, and large trees were installed to create a more pleasing effect.

The rear yard had not yet been landscaped, because President Brooks was still hoping to build a back porch. It is interesting that most of the rear shutters are closed.

In the fall of 1928, before the house was completed, President Brooks attempted to add the planned back porch that had been eliminated to keep within the strict budget. Except for the porch in the lower west wing, there was no outdoor connection of the house to the landscape. The view of the woods of Pullen Park behind the house was a compelling vista. President Brooks requested that Upjohn send him a sketch for a "simple and not too expensive" rear porch that he would construct out of his own funds. Upjohn sent drawings for a porch that would not "look disjointed with the house. You can readily understand that anything that would stick straight out from the back of this building is out of key with the building itself." [12] The president wrote back that "we held up any improvement in the rear until these plans could come, but since they have arrived and I find that I cannot afford the expense, we have had the campus force level the land so that it will be presentable," adding wistfully that the porch could perhaps be built the following year. [13] Upjohn's porch design does not survive, and neither the Brookses nor any of the other residents of the house ever added a back porch. A porch along the garden elevation would have emphasized a role of equal importance to the façade on the Hillsborough Street frontage. The house wanted a rear porch because it was intended to face in both directions.

After the decision not to add a rear porch, the back yard was landscaped with retaining walls at the outer edges of the main block, steps leading down a paved walkway, and a driveway that extends behind the house. The awning sheltered the wide rear entrance from the southern sun.

Notes

1 Jennifer Martin, Sarah Woodard, Clay Griffith, and Cynthia de Miranda, "Maiden Lane Historic District," National Register Nomination (Raleigh: N.C. Historic Preservation Office, 2005); Keith Nichols, Dave Pond, and Matthew Robbins, "History of the Chancellor's Residence," *This Red House* (blog), http://web.ncsu.edu/this-red-house/history.

2 M. Ruth Little, *The Town and Gown Architecture of Chapel Hill, North Carolina, 1795–1975*, 42–3, 148–9. The first house has disappeared.

3 Minutes of the Building Committee, Board of Trustees, August 17, 1923, Office of the Chancellor Records, UA002.001.001, box 1, folder 10. No plans for a residence designed by Nelson survive; likely the project was deferred before Nelson started work.

4 Hobart Upjohn, memorandum to his office, June 21, 1927, Office of the Chancellor Records, UA002.001.001, box 3, folder 5.

5 Ibid.

6 Ibid.

7 Margaret S. Smith, "Charles Barton Keen," in *North Carolina Architects & Builders*; Catherine Bishir, interview by the author, January 30, 2013.

8 Hobart Upjohn to Dr. E.C. Brooks, July 5, 1927, Office of the Chancellor Records, UA002.001.001, box 3, folder 5.

9 Michelle Michael, email correspondence with the author, October 15, 2012. The Rankin House stands on North Cool Spring Street in Fayetteville, N.C.

10 E.C. Brooks, letter to Hobart Upjohn, September 2, 1927; Otto Langmann, letter to E.C. Brooks, September 10, 1927, Office of the Chancellor Records, UA002.001.001, box 3, folder 13.

11 Correspondence between Upjohn, Brooks, Jewell-Riddell Company, and others, September–October 1927, Office of the Chancellor Records, UA002.001.001, box 3, folder 13; "Many Changes Occurring around the Campus of N.C. State College," *Alumni News (North Carolina State College)*, November 1927, 4–5.

12 Hobart Upjohn, letter to Dr. E.C. Brooks, September 22, 1928, Office of the Chancellor Records, UA002.001.001, box 3. The proposed porch plans have not been located.

13 E.C. Brooks, letter to Hobart Upjohn, October 1, 1928, Office of the Chancellor Records, UA002.001.001, box 3.

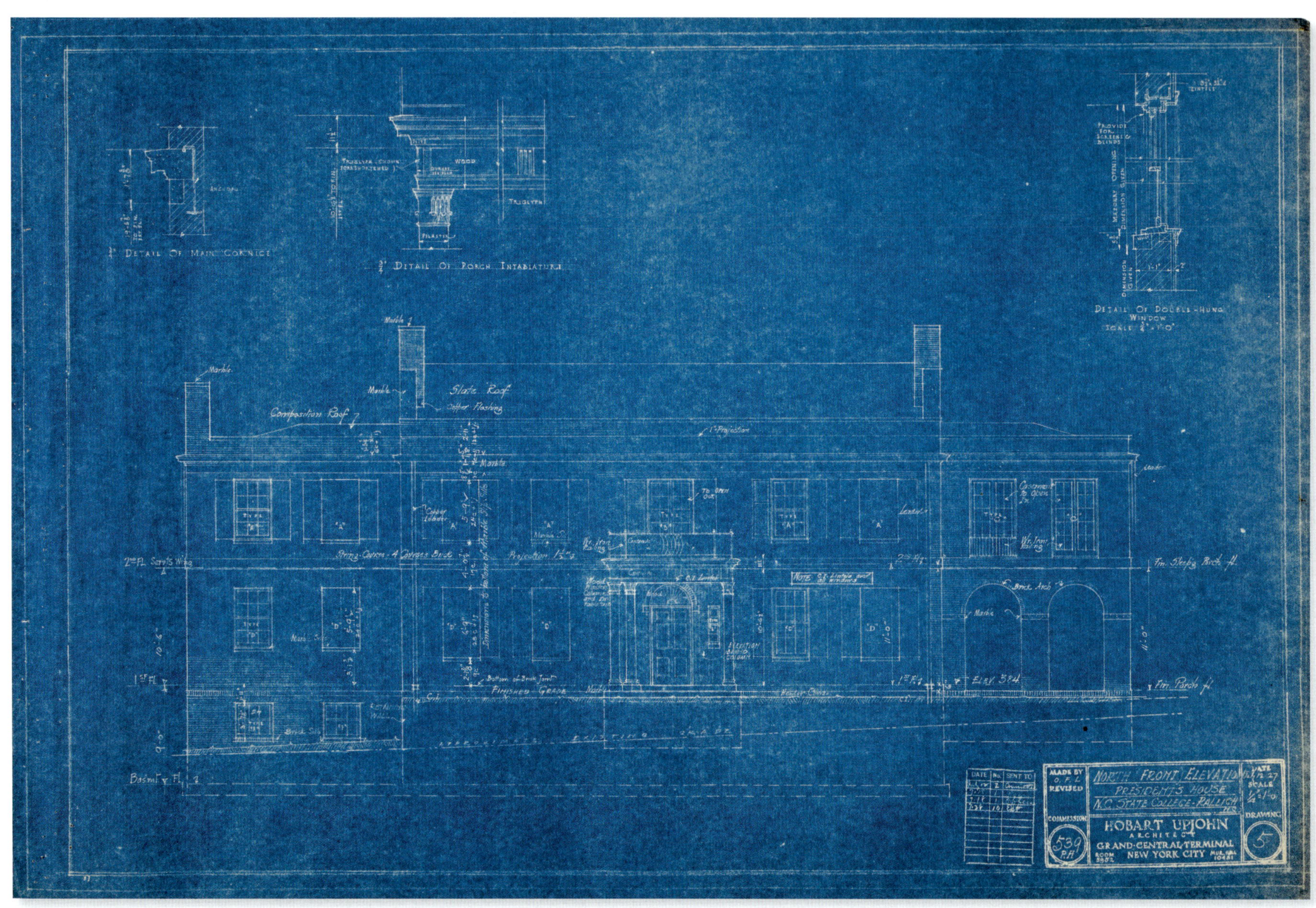

President's House, front elevation. Hobart Upjohn blueprint, 1927. NCSU Libraries Special Collections Research Center.

President's House, rear elevation. Hobart Upjohn blueprint, 1927. NCSU Libraries Special Collections Research Center.

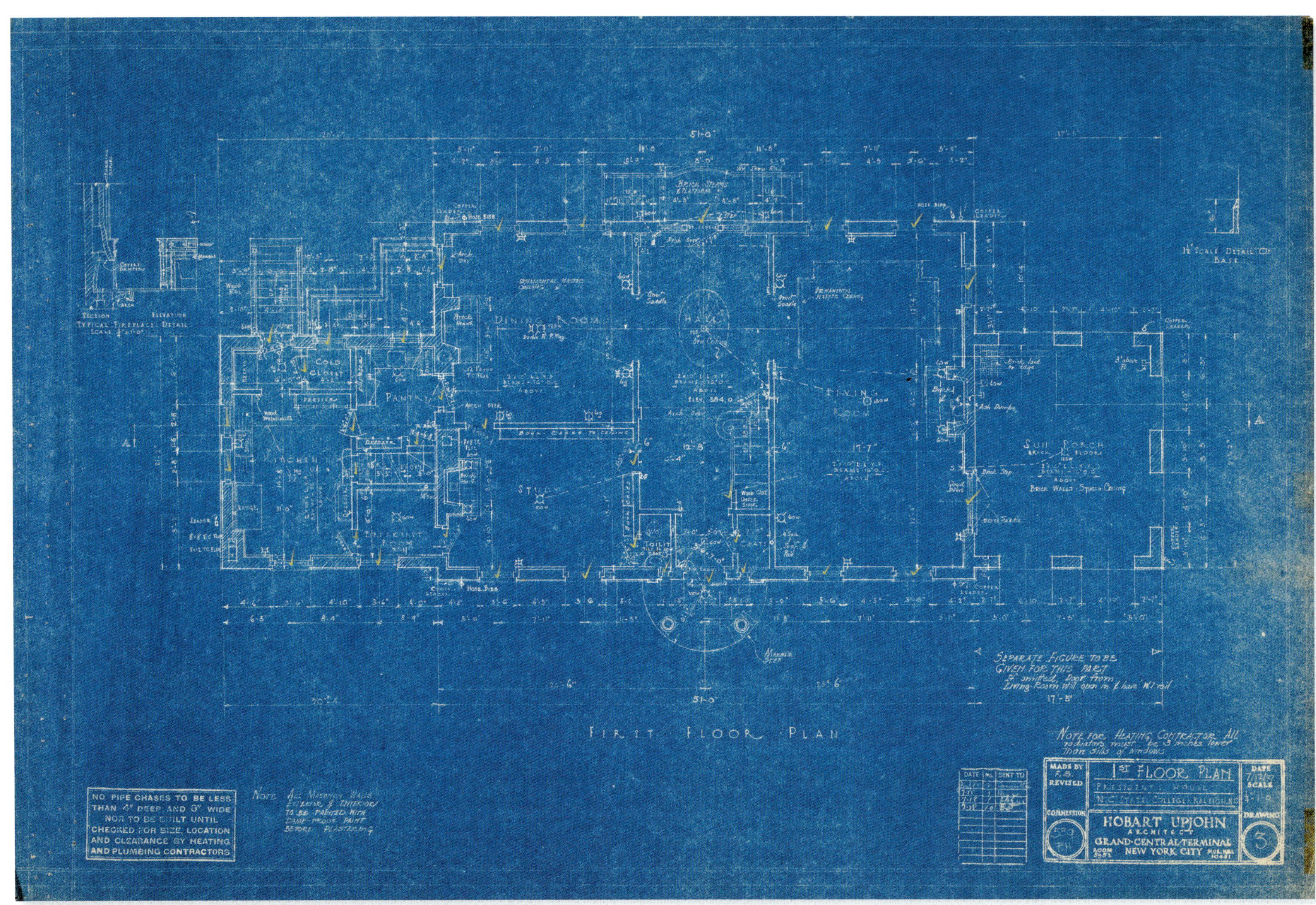

President's House, first floor plan. Hobart Upjohn blueprint, 1927. NCSU Libraries Special Collections Research Center.

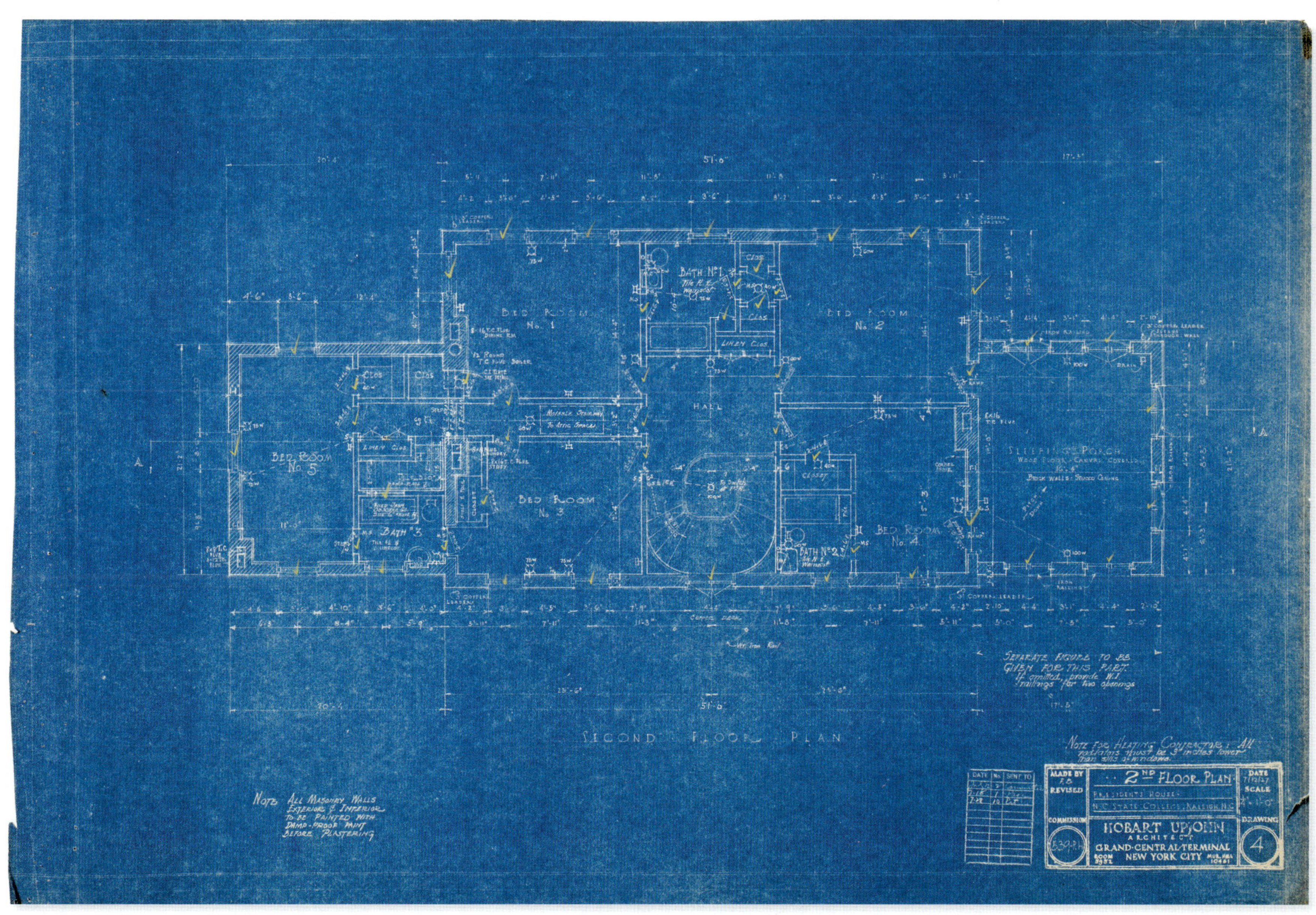

President's House, second floor plan. Hobart Upjohn blueprint, 1927. NCSU Libraries Special Collections Research Center.

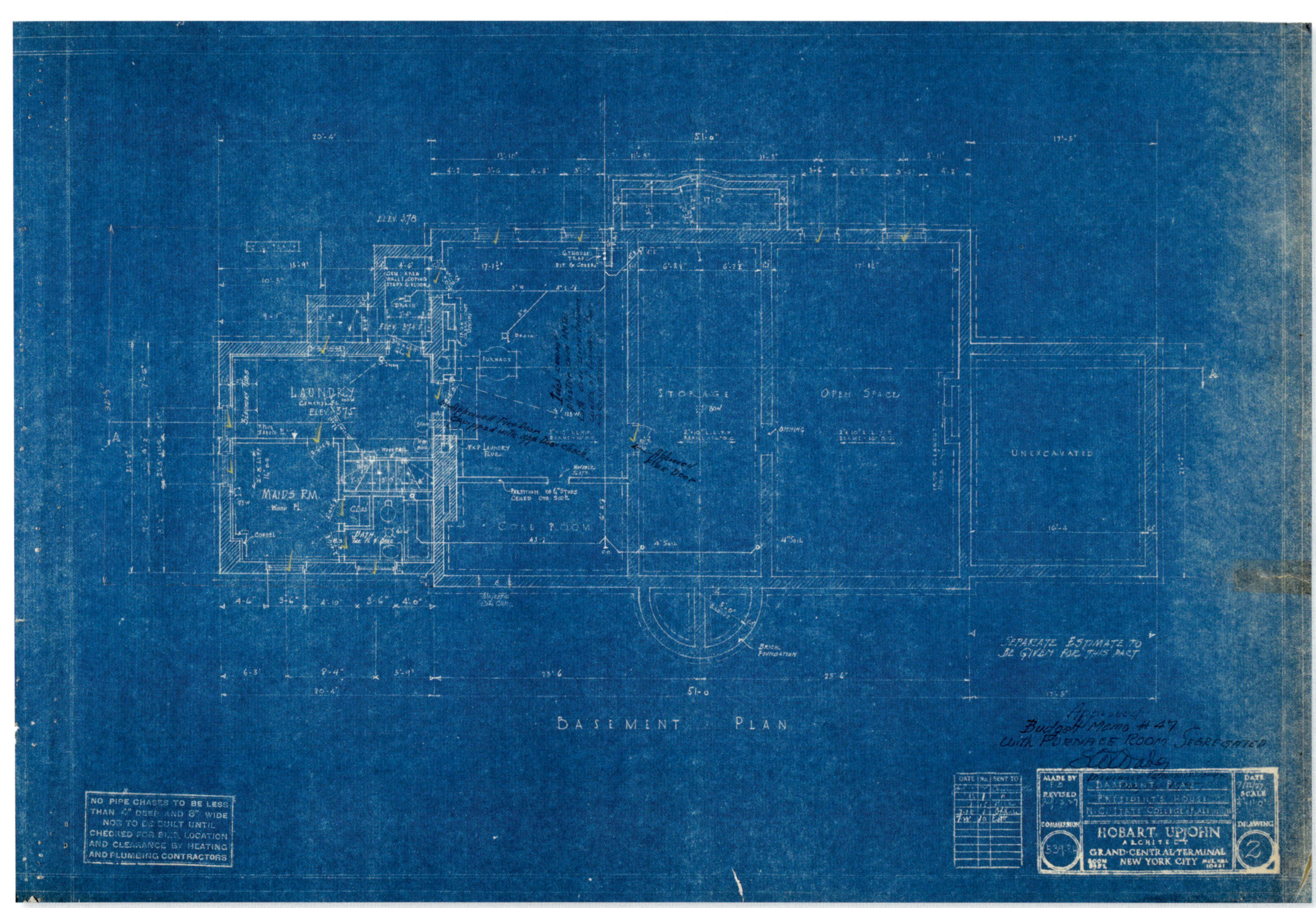

President's House, basement plan. Hobart Upjohn blueprint, 1927. NCSU Libraries Special Collections Research Center.

President's Residence, center hall looking toward the rear garden and Pullen Park. Photograph by Craig McDuffie, 2012.

UNIVERSITY'S LIVING ROOM

Each family varied in size, in their styles of entertainment, and in their interactions with the domestic staff who were indispensable to the functioning of the residence as the center of hospitality for the college.

CHAPTER FOUR

NC State University's Living Room

The reflecting ball of the State College residence carries dim outlines of hundreds of parties, dinners, meetings, open houses, teas, ceremonies, holiday celebrations, and other special occasions for the college and for the families who have lived there over the years. Each family varied in size, in their styles of entertainment, and in their interactions with the domestic staff who were indispensable to the functioning of the residence as the center of hospitality for the college. The official residence became "the university's living room," as William C. Friday, president of the UNC system, once remarked about the Carolina Inn in Chapel Hill.

President Eugene C. and Ida Brooks (1923–1934)

Because Eugene and Ida Brooks had diligently overseen the design of the house, they were likely comfortable in their new home. The cozy room left of the front door designated by the architect as a study was used by the Brookses as a den. It was originally fitted with bookcases, and a door to the left of the fireplace accessed the breakfast room. The breakfast room was later converted to a pantry and the door removed. Ida slept in the master bedroom over the living room, while in nice weather Eugene preferred the sleeping porch. Eugene used the smallest upstairs bedroom, No. 4, adjacent to the sleeping porch, as his study.

Their three children, Eugene Brooks Jr., Sara, and Martha, were grown by the time their parents moved into the President's Residence, but they visited often along with their own children. When their granddaughter, Luzette Callum of Greensboro, visited the "college house," as it was known, she stayed in the bedroom over the kitchen. Her mother, Martha, would stay in "Bedroom No. 3," and their maid, Annie Mae Fuller, slept in Luzette's bedroom. Luzette enjoyed playing around the eighteenth-century Andrew Johnson House behind the house.[1] The little Johnson House had been moved from downtown Raleigh to Pullen Park in the early twentieth century and remained there until 1975, when it was relocated to Mordecai Park near downtown Raleigh. Johnson, a Raleigh native, served as vice president under

ABOVE: Sara Brooks at her wedding to Edwin Pullen, November 9, 1929, in the President's Residence. Courtesy of Sara's daughter Sally Kelly, Winston-Salem, N.C.

FACING PAGE: Tea service in the home's dining room when the Woodsons lived there. Susan Woodson inherited it from her parents. Photograph by Craig McDuffie, 2012.

LEFT: Luzette Callum, the Brooks's three-year-old granddaughter, sitting on the front steps during one of her frequent visits to the President's Residence, about 1929. Courtesy of Luzette Callum Brown.

RIGHT: Ida ("Idee") Brooks and her granddaughter Luzette at the President's Residence, ca. 1929. Courtesy of Luzette Callum Brown.

Abraham Lincoln and filled out his term from the time of Lincoln's assassination in the spring of 1865 until 1869.[2]

Born in Greene County in 1871, Eugene Brooks had attended Trinity College (later Duke University), and married Ida Sapp of Kernersville, North Carolina, in the late 1890s. He had become a decisive figure in North Carolina education by working his way up the educational ladder—teacher, principal, superintendent of city schools, deputy superintendent of the North Carolina Department of Public Instruction, founder and head of the department of education at Trinity College from 1907–1919, and finally state superintendent of public instruction, where he established local tax districts for schools, consolidated school buildings, standardized teacher credentials, curriculums, and salaries, and upgraded textbooks. Among Brooks's publications were *The Story of Cotton and the Development of the Cotton States,* 1911; *The Story of Corn and the Westward Migration,* 1916; *Woodrow Wilson as President,* 1916; and a teacher's magazine he edited for seventeen years.[3] In his new office in the President's Residence after 1928, Brooks continued former President Riddick's work to implement the Zook Report reorganization and to develop the newly organized schools of Agriculture, Education, Science and Business, Textiles, and Engineering.

During their six years in the President's Residence, the Brooks family entertained privately as well as held official college events. In an important early family event in the house, Sara Brooks was married to Edwin Tilmon Pullen, a descendant of Richard Stanhope Pullen, on November 9, 1929, with a reception afterward. Sara and her husband, who worked in the insurance business, lived in Winston-Salem,

that their reliance on the money crops of cotton and tobacco had cast an "evil enchantment" upon the state that prevented farmers from using their acres to grow the corn, wheat, potatoes, beans, may, cattle, hogs, and poultry that could actually feed and sustain them.[8]

State College's agriculture, textile, and engineering programs, extension classes, and the county agricultural agencies promoted the gospel of self-sufficiency for farmers and families through crop diversity, scientific agriculture, and technological ingenuity. The Agricultural Extension Service, formally headquartered at the college since 1914, provided federal funds for extension activities. Home demonstration agents distributed the latest in scientific information and home economics, encouraged home gardens, and taught safe canning procedures. By 1937 all one hundred counties had an extension agent. The 4-H clubs were an important conduit of outreach, and the annual 4-H summer course at State College was well attended. The Textile School promoted its cloth through fashion shows held in cooperation with Meredith College, the nearby women's college.[9]

In 1931, to save money during the Depression, UNC-Chapel Hill, State College, and the Women's College at Greensboro were consolidated under a single administration, making Dr. Frank Porter Graham of UNC the new president of the consolidated university and demoting President Brooks to vice president and later dean of administration. The Depression's financial toll reduced State College's enrollment from nearly 2,000 in 1929 to approximately 1,500 by 1933. President Brooks continued to lead the college until 1934, when he turned over his college residence to new administrator John W. Harrelson.[10]

ABOVE: The State College Engineers Club celebrates St. Patrick, the patron saint of engineering, who drove the snakes out of Ireland, at a St. Patrick's Day parade on Fayetteville Street in Raleigh in the 1930s. NCSU Libraries Special Collections Research Center.

LEFT: Harrelsons in the rear garden of the residence. Harrelson Photo Album, NCSU Libraries Special Collection Research Center.

RIGHT: The College Court Pharmacy anchored the small campus business district at the corner of Hillsborough Street and Oberlin Road in 1945. The Chancellor's Residence is behind the trees on the right. Hillsborough Street, 1945. Albert Barden, photographer. State Archives of North Carolina.

Dean of Administration/Chancellor John William Harrelson and Elizabeth Harrelson (1934–1953)

John William Harrelson (1885–1955), from Cleveland County, North Carolina, led State College through most of the Great Depression, World War II, and well into the postwar recovery. Harrelson graduated from State College with an undergraduate engineering degree (1909) and a master's degree in mechanical engineering (1915). His military service during World War I led to his nickname of "colonel," which he used throughout his life. From 1929 to 1933 the colonel headed the North Carolina Department of Conservation and Development, then became head of the State College Department of Mathematics in 1933. The following year he became the chief executive, known as the dean of administration following the college's absorption into the Consolidated University of North Carolina. Colonel Harrelson moved into the college residence in 1934 and married Miss Elizabeth Connor the following year. By 1940, Harrelson's seventy-four-year-old mother Ellen lived in the residence as well.[11]

Campus improvements, which had stopped by 1931 due to the Depression, resumed in the late 1930s. From 1936 to 1939 Public Works Administration (PWA) and Works Progress Administration (WPA) funds of the New Deal allowed construction of several more of Upjohn and Manning's master plan buildings—Withers Hall (chemistry); Becton and Berry halls, that aligned with Bagwell Dormitory of 1925 to form a court; and the Field House at Riddick Field. The Memorial Tower, begun in 1921, was completed in 1937, and several more dormitories and classroom buildings—Nelson Hall (textiles); and Mangum Hall (agricultural engineering, later renamed David Clark Laboratory) were also built from the New Deal funds. State College architecture professor Ross Shumaker and his assistant Jesse Page, with consultation from Hobart Upjohn, designed most of the new buildings.[12]

A Haven of Hospitality during World War II

Elizabeth Harrelson moved into the president's house in 1935, and despite the Depression and subsequent war she made it a haven of hospitality and beauty. The progress of the late 1930s was interrupted by World War II. Enrollment at State College peaked in 1942 and dropped to 700 students by 1945. The campus took on the aspect of a military base, training 23,628 military personnel and laying the foundation for a giant leap in technological education based on wartime research and collaboration with private manufacturers when the war was over.[13] The house was always open to students, faculty, and friends of the college, leading to the observation that "the individual who has not experienced the cordial hospitality of the Harrelson home has missed one of the finest things State College has to offer."[14] The powder blue paint scheme and red patterned curtains in the residence's living room, shown in the *Agromeck* photograph, were likely selected by Mrs. Harrelson. The original decorative plaster ceiling molding was removed in later years.

ABOVE: Chancellor's Residence, living room. The Agromeck *(1943) published this photograph of a formal reception in the living room of the Chancellor's Residence. The caption, "Gentlemen, we give you the Ladies! . . . it is for them we will fight, live and become better men," is a reminder that the fairer sex was much revered at the male college, especially during the uncertainty of war. Most college students were wearing military uniforms rather than tuxedos.*

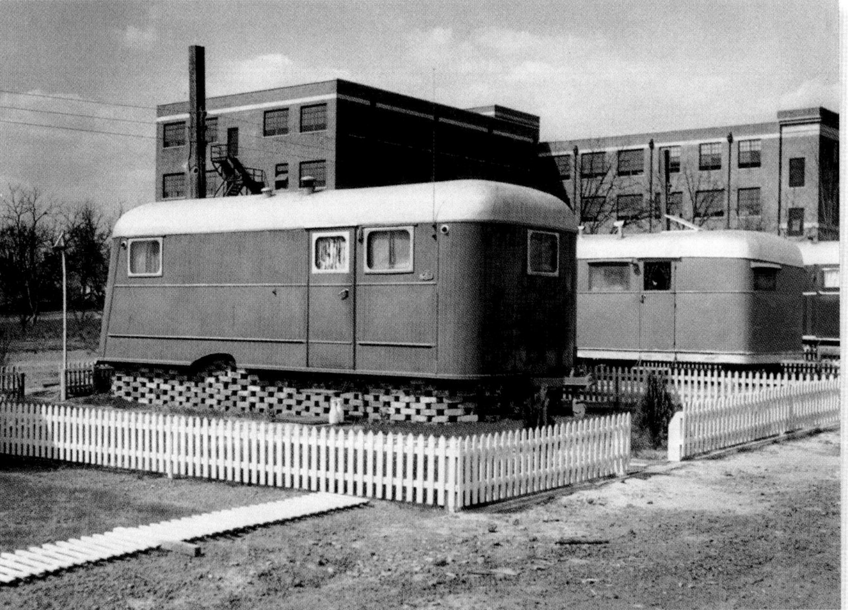

In 1945 the title of the adminstrative head changed from Dean of Administration to Chancellor. After the war, military veterans, funded by the G.I. Bill of Rights, flooded the campus. In fall 1947 over 5,000 students enrolled. Many of these were married men, leading to a scramble to provide victory village–type housing for the married students and surplus barracks housing for the single veterans. Colonel Harrelson led the college through the later years of the Depression, through World War II, and supervised the establishment of the School of Design in 1948 and the School of Forestry in 1950.

Chancellor Carey Hoyt Bostian and Neita Bostian (1953–1959)

Carey Hoyt Bostian carried State College through the remaining years of its 1950s boom. Bostian, raised in Rowan County and educated at Catawba College, North Carolina, and the University of Pittsburgh, taught genetics and served as director of instruction for the State College School of Agriculture. During his leadership from 1953 to 1959 he became known as the "reorganization chancellor" for restoring the authority of his office following a period when the deans of individual schools had reported directly to the president of the Consolidated University. He and his wife Neita had three sons, twins Floyd and K. Eugene and the youngest son R. Lee, all students at State College who lived at the Chancellor's Residence. Floyd and K. Eugene studied agronomy, the science of crop production. Floyd

FACING PAGE, TOP LEFT: Dean of Administration Harrelson, known as Colonel Harrelson for his World War I service, stands in the center at this 1940 ROTC ceremony. NCSU Libraries Special Collections Research Center.

FACING PAGE, TOP RIGHT: Members of the Scabbard and Blade college military honor society, 1942–1943, at State College. NCSU Libraries Special Collections Research Center.

FACING PAGE, BOTTOM LEFT: Court of North Carolina. Temporary barracks and Quonset huts were erected in the Court of North Carolina for housing and classrooms after World War II. These stood into the 1950s. 1948 photograph. NCSU Libraries Special Collections Research Center.

FACING PAGE, BOTTOM RIGHT: Trailwood Village (married student housing). Trailwood married housing village, with 115 trailers, opened in 1946. The other temporary married housing villages at the college were Vetville and Westhaven. NCSU Libraries Special Collections Research Center.

THIS PAGE: Erdahl-Cloyd Union. The Student Union, completed in 1952 from a bold modern design by the firm of Raleigh architect William Deitrick, was likely the work of Matthew Nowicki while associated with Deitrick. The free-standing building was later incorporated into D.H. Hill Library and is now known as the Erdahl-Cloyd Wing. Nowicki also designed the internationally famous Dorton Arena shortly before his death in 1950.[15] William H. Deitrick architectural firm. NCSU Libraries Special Collections Research Center.

FACING PAGE, TOP LEFT: By the 1950s ivy had been allowed to climb the Chancellor's Residence, as it had other college buildings. Harrelson Photo Album. NCSU Libraries Special Collections Research Center.

FACING PAGE, TOP RIGHT: Chancellor's Residence, living room. The Harrelsons decorated the residence with an elegant mixture of heirlooms and contemporary furniture. Colonel Harrelson's portrait commands the living room in this 1950s view inside the Chancellor's House. Harrelson Photo Album. NCSU Libraries Special Collections Research Center.

FACING PAGE, BOTTOM LEFT: Elizabeth Harrelson had the brick wall and fountain erected to enclose the rear garden, likely during the 1950s. Chancellor's Residence, rear view. Harrelson Photo Album. NCSU Libraries Special Collections Research Center.

FACING PAGE, BOTTOM RIGHT: Chancellors Carey Bostian and John Harrelson with their wives, Neita and Elizabeth, in 1954. NCSU Libraries Special Collections Research Center.

was married, and his wife lived at the residence as well. Chancellor Bostian was an avid gardner who had cultivated vegetables, fruit trees, and grape vines at his home on Dixie Trail in Raleigh, and he maintained his garden even after moving into the college residence. [16]

Bostian presided over the construction of ten new buildings needed to handle the college's post-war growth: the new D.H. Hill Library, Gardner Hall (biological sciences); Broughton Hall (mechanical engineering); Kilgore Hall (horticulture and forestry); Scott Hall (poultry sciences); Weaver Laboratories (biological and agriculture engineering); Grinnells Animal Health Laboratories; Burlington Engineering Laboratories (the first nuclear reactor used exclusively for the peacetime study of atomic energy); the Erdahl-Cloyd College Union; Bragaw Hall (the first modernist-style dormitory); and the expansion of the original infirmary into the Alumni Memorial Building. In 1954 the college awarded the first doctorate in nuclear engineering in the United States.

Bostian was proud of his efforts to open lines of communication through his weekly meeting with student government leaders and to integrate African Americans into the student body. The first African Americans enrolled as graduate students in 1953, and the first four undergraduate students (Edward Carson, Manuel Crockett, Irwin Holmes, and Walter Holmes) enrolled in 1956. Bostian was a quiet but firm integrationist. When Walter Holmes attempted to become a member of the college marching band, Bostian resisted outside pressure and allowed him to join the band. In the late 1950s, the band unanimously decided to boycott a football game at Clemson, South Carolina because they were told that their two black members would not be allowed to play. Bostian recalled that "although it is a little thing, it made me feel very good that our students felt that way about it." [17]

Another progressive initiative of Chancellor Bostian's tenure was his role in the establishment of the Research Triangle Park between Raleigh, Durham, and Chapel Hill, now one of the most prominent high-tech research and development centers in the United States. Sociologist Howard W. Odum at UNC-Chapel Hill proposed the idea in the early 1950s. Bostian and various deans worked closely with university officials at Chapel Hill to make the research and manufacturing campus a reality. In 1958 the Research Triangle Institute, the first institution to locate in the newly formed research park, was established by State College, UNC-Chapel Hill, and Duke University. [18]

ABOVE: John Caldwell with his wife Catherine and children Helen, Alice, Andrew, and Charles in 1960. NCSU Libraries Special Collections Research Center.

Chancellor John Tyler Caldwell (1959–1975) and Catherine Caldwell (1959–1961)

In 1959 John Tyler Caldwell became the eighth administrative head of State College and played a major role in the college's evolution from a state college to a university during the next sixteen years. The political science professor, who was raised in Mississippi, had previously been president of the University of Arkansas. His service during the turbulent Sixties involved him in the big issues of the era: Civil Rights, the later years of the McCarthy witch hunt for Communists, the Vietnam War, and women's education. In 1963, when Consolidated University administrators renamed the institution "University of North Carolina at Raleigh," State College students, faculty, and alumni were outraged. Fraternities picketed the Chancellor's Residence. In 1965 a mutually palatable "NC State University at Raleigh" was finalized. One example of Caldwell's ability to forge a warm bond with the students occurred at a commencement during his tenure. After the honors students were recognized, Dr. Caldwell said, "Now I want all the students here who are graduating with a C average to stand, because I want to tell the rest of you students some of you are going to be working for these C average students." Caldwell felt strongly that dependability, common sense, practicality, and determination were also important components of success.[19]

Chancellor Caldwell continued the peaceful and orderly integration of African American students and faculty into the institution, contributing to the university's growing national and international reputation. Although many Raleigh merchants and landlords resisted integration, he spoke in 1960 to area businesses urging the integration of public facilities, including restaurants. One of Caldwell's fondest memories as chancellor was the day in 1963 when Mr. Baxley, owner of Baxley's Restaurant, located at the corner of Hillsborough Street and Maiden Lane, walked into his office and said, "My wife and I have been thinking a lot about this matter of serving blacks in our restaurants.... We prayed about it a lot this weekend and I have come in here … to tell you that from now on, we are going to serve anybody who walks in our doors and we are going to be happy doing it."[20] NC State University's steady progress in integration resulted in the enrollment of 1,657 black students by 1982.[21]

Assemblages of large crowds of students, angry or afraid about issues of the turbulent Sixties, sometimes gathered on the front lawn of the Chancellor's Residence to express their frustrations to Chancellor Caldwell. His son Andy Caldwell recalled that his father would always go out and talk with the students, usually with good results. One such issue at North Carolina college campuses during the era was the treatment of African American non-academic employees. On February 28, 1969, the Society for Afro-American Culture at the university organized a torchlight parade at the Chancellor's Residence to highlight the degrading conditions of black campus workers, especially the female housekeepers in men's dormitories. The leader of the janitors and housekeepers was Eddie Davis, a union organizer who was employed as a janitor.[22] Both the McCarthy era repression of free speech and the Vietnam War also incited NC State University students. The "Speaker Ban Law" passed in 1963 that forbade any known communists or anyone who pleaded the Fifth Amendment regarding communism from speaking on campuses of the Consolidated University was extremely unpopular with university students. Chancellor Caldwell opposed it as well, labeling it "A Berlin Wall of the Mind." In 1968 the law was declared unconstitutional.[23] Protests at NC State University against the Vietnam War began in 1967 and reached their

ABOVE: Caldwell family, ca. 1968. Left to right: Chuck Caldwell, Melanie Erskine, Helen Caldwell, Chancellor John T. Caldwell, holding Shirene, Carol Erskine Caldwell, Alice Caldwell, Carol Case Erskine, Andy Caldwell. Caldwell Family Photo Album.

r cooking by heart

Mrs. Ruffin and Mrs. John T. Caldwell consult on week's menu

together they plan meals often using Mrs. Ruffin's recipes

Graduates honored tonight

Five women have been selected as outstanding graduates of Household Assistance, Inc., and will be awarded certificates at the alumnae meeting tonight at Chavis Heights Recreation Center.

They are Lois Rowland, housekeeper for the president of Meredith College; Hattie Ruffin, housekeeper for the chancellor of North Carolina State University; Valeen King Lanier, head of maintenance at St. Augustine's College; Glenora Parham, president of a private home maintenance business, and Sara Battle, day care aide with the West Raleigh Presbyterian Church.

Household Assistance, Inc., is an organization formed in 1968 and run by a board made up of women employers and graduates of the course who are currently engaged in domestic work.

Purpose of the program is to raise the status of domestic work through providing on - the - job training and educating employers to "dignify" the work with higher wages and benefits.

The group has published a code of standards which are presented to employers and employes at the end of the course.

A grant from the Human Development Campaign of the Catholic Diocese of Raleigh will fund the fifth class of Household Assistance, Inc.

Registration for the classes, which will be taught by Mrs. Charles D. Mooney, home economist, will be held from 9 a.m. to 12 noon Nov. 5 at the East Hargett Street Y. W. C. A.

The clsses will be held at the Meredith College Alumnae House from 6:45 p.m. to 8:45 p.m. Nov. 7 through 10, and Nov 14 through 17.

Corn Pudding Ruffin

- 4 eggs
- ½ cup sugar
- 2 tablespoons plain flour
- 2 cups milk
- 1 can shoe peg corn
- 2 tablespoons melted butter
- Drop of vanilla

Drain corn. Beat eggs until light. Add sugar, flour, milk. Combine with corn. Add butter. Pour into casserole. Bake at 300 degrees for 1½ hours.

"Mrs. Ruffin Knows Her Cooking By Heart," *Raleigh Times*, October 11, 1972.

LEFT: Hattie Ruffin and Carol Erskine Caldwell planning the week's menus at the Chancellor's Residence, 1972. Caldwell Family Photo Album.

peak in 1969–1970. Chancellor Caldwell went to numerous assemblies and workshops on campus to allow the students to voice their frustrations.[24]

Chancellor Caldwell supported the rising enrollment of women from 197 in 1961 to 2,097 in 1969. Although a few female students studied at State College beginning in the 1920s, coeds were rare until after World War II. Before Caldwell's tenure, conditions for women at the college were deplorable: there was no on-campus housing and very few women's restroom facilities in the largely male institution. Watauga Hall was remodeled as the first women's dormitory in 1964; the second women's dormitory, Alexander Residence Hall, opened in 1967. By 1983 thirty-five percent of the student body was female.[25]

The chancellor and his wife Catherine had four children: Alice, Chuck, Andy, and Helen. The Caldwells used the sleeping porch as their bedroom and had a sunroom added behind the kitchen to serve as a playroom for the children. The children's early life in the Chancellor's Residence has remained vivid in their memories. One night the doorbell rang and Andy, in his pajamas, answered the door to see William Friday, the UNC system president, standing on the doorstep waiting to see his father.[26]

Chancellor John Tyler Caldwell (1959–1975) and Carol Erskine Caldwell (1963–1975)

ABOVE: Chancellor's Residence, ca. 1970. Caldwell Family Photo Album.

Chancellor Caldwell, widowed in 1961, married Carol Erskine of Wisconsin in 1963. Carol had been introduced to Dr. Caldwell by her sister-in-law Ginny Harris, who lived in Raleigh. Ginny was the sister of Carol's deceased husband. Carol moved into the Chancellor's Residence with her two daughters, swelling the household to six children. The dinner table was crowded with children as well as guests.

Hattie Ruffin, a new housekeeper who would be an important presence for the next twenty-six years, came to the residence along with Carol Caldwell. Mrs. Ruffin, an experienced cook, had worked for Ginny Harris. Ginny offered to give her the opportunity to work at the Chancellor's Residence. At the time, a male cook worked at the residence, so at first Mrs. Ruffin cooked only on the weekends. Before long she became the full-time cook and housekeeper. Carol Caldwell appreciated that Mrs. Ruffin's food and personality created an easy Southern atmosphere at the residence. "The wonderful thing about Hattie is that she loves a party. . . . Coming from the North and marrying a Southerner who was accustomed to Southern cooking, I was at a real loss when it came to cooking foods like black-eyed peas and grits. . . . Dr. Caldwell likes nothing better than to ride around the campus, pick up a couple of students and bring them home for dinner. So we have to be ready for that sort of thing too. . . . Hattie is the one who gives the first impression of the hospitality we want people to feel when they come to our home. She often answers the telephone and the door and her warmth is an essential part of the feeling we want to convey."[27]

ABOVE: Harwell Harris at his drafting table, 1960s. NCSU Libraries Special Collections Research Center.

Harwell Hamilton Harris at the Chancellor's Residence

In 1975 university trustees studied whether to replace the chancellor's residence. A newspaper article about the study noted that "periodically, swarms of professors, deans, students and alumni gather in the immaculate formal garden, or crowd into the small downstairs rooms. It's a long-standing tradition that the chancellor entertains university personnel frequently in his home. Yet it's at those times that the seemingly large house shrinks remarkably." The trustees commissioned Harwell Hamilton Harris, an internationally famous architect teaching at the NC State University School of Design, to design a new residence. Harris noted that the house is a tool that the chancellor uses to further his work, but it "was designed as just … a private home … there is no separation, for entertainment purposes, between the chancellor and his family's private and public lives." Ultimately the trustees authorized a $137,000 renovation that included new HVAC systems, plumbing and wiring, insulation, waterproofing, updated bathrooms, and refurbished grounds. Harris served as consulting architect and helped incoming first lady Marly Thomas select paint colors for shutters and interior spaces as she planned her family's move into the residence. (Newspaper article, "1903 Hillsborough St.," by Kim Devins, Thomas Family Scrapbook.)

Even when an event for as many as three hundred people took place at the residence, Mrs. Ruffin rose to the occasion by calling in her good friends or several students to help out with the food. Inside the house, she arranged fresh flowers from the roses and other flowers in the rear garden. For receptions she often served homemade pound cake and homemade peach ice cream. In 1963 the editor of the *Daily Times* of London and his wife were guests; another night two young Formosan students came for a picnic in the garden. Her seasoned collard greens, fried chicken, corn pudding, and biscuits catered to Chancellor Caldwell's Mississippi palate.

As the Caldwell children remembered, Hattie Ruffin would fry up a huge batch of chicken on Fridays, laying it on brown paper bags along the kitchen countertops to drain, so that the children would have enough to eat during the weekend. She also baked dozens of chocolate chip cookies to tide them over until she returned on Mondays. She good-naturedly kept the house functioning. When Alice Caldwell took over the upstairs hallway for her insect collection, a project for a biology class, Mrs. Ruffin eventually called a halt and made her move it to another location. Andy recalled how she would chide his father for staining his clothes as he walked home from Holladay Hall. Wearing his white shirt, tie, and suit, he would stop at the persimmon tree beside the garage and eat a fruit, then pick a tomato from the garden, salt it with the shaker that he kept on the garage window sill, and eat. When he walked into the house with juice dripping down his tie and shirt, Hattie would fuss, "Dr. Caldwell, look at what you have done to your clothes!" [28]

Chancellor Joab L. Thomas and Marly Thomas (1976-1981)

After the turbulence of Caldwell's era, the student body had quieted, allowing Joab Langston Thomas, the next chancellor, to be more low key and less visible as he fine-tuned the growing university. Thomas, an Alabama native and Harvard-trained botanist, assumed leadership of the university in 1976 after serving as administrator of student affairs at the University of Alabama. He was attracted to NC State University because it was a first-rate research university with strengths in food, energy, environment, and shelter. "My goal was to make this institution stronger and better at what it did, but not to become elitist." He worked to overcome what he called the inferiority complex of the university, in which people "had grown accustomed to looking over their shoulder at a tall shadow about twenty-eight miles to the west." [29] Chancellor Thomas took great pride in the university's extension offices and their transmittal of technologies such as new species of tobacco that resisted disease, bulk curing barns for tobacco, and hybrid corn. The university helped increase the productivity of animal and grain industries that were of paramount importance for the North Carolina economy.

Thomas's tenure saw gains in women's participation and in university outreach. Enrollment exceeded 20,000, with a greater percentage of women students and of women faculty. Bob Tilman, dean of Humanities and Social Sciences, pioneered a program of sending out humanists to various counties for lectures and workshops. The North Carolina–Japan Center and the School of Veterinary Medicine were established. The Jane S. McKimmon Center for Extension and Continuing Education, a national model for short refresher courses in continuing education, was built in 1976 for the University Extension Service. The Micro-Electronics Center at Research Triangle Park was

BELOW: Joab and Marly and the children (clockwise from left: Jennifer, Catherine, David, and Frances (seated) in the Chancellor's Residence following the September 1976 installation ceremony. Thomas Family Scrapbook.

LEFT: Hattie Ruffin working in the kitchen during a Christmas party in the residence in 1980. Thomas Family Scrapbook.

RIGHT: The NC State University Woman's Club's Christmas coffee, in the dining room of the Chancellor's Residence in 1977. Christmas decorations were created by the members. Thomas Family Scrapbook.

developed with the help of the university. Dr. Thomas's interest and support of college athletics was particularly admired. He rarely missed a football game, supported the women's athletic program, and felt that athletics was important for the individual development of students.[30]

The Thomas family, including youngsters Catherine, David, Jennifer, and Frances, moved into the chancellor's house in 1976. Frances's pet mouse Emily was mentioned in the *Raleigh Times* because it flew to Raleigh in a cage carried by acting chancellor Jackson Rigney instead of riding in the family car from Atlanta. The family had been living in Tuscaloosa where Thomas was the vice president of student affairs at the University of Alabama.[31] Hattie Ruffin, still the housekeeper, ensured that the hospitality of the Caldwell era would continue under the Thomases. She gave them a tour when they first arrived. "These are my tablecloths … these are my napkins," she said as she showed off the linens used for dinners at the residence.[32]

Marly Thomas had an event at the house about once a week, including pre-game gatherings for sports events, staff and faculty Christmas parties, student leader get-togethers, and teas and

dinners. She did the grocery shopping herself, concentrating on fresh foods in season, then she and Hattie prepared all the food. May—graduation month—was always the busiest time. In May 1978 she entertained 1,500 people at various luncheons, receptions, teas, and dinners in the residence. An article in the Raleigh *News and Observer* included three of Marly's favorite party dishes: escalloped eggplant, curried shrimp with noodle-coconut topping, and orange blossom cake with ambrosia filling.[33]

Three of the most memorable parties that Marly hosted involved a famous musician and visitors from the Middle East. In February 1976 American composer Aaron Copland visited NC State University to help the choral groups produce a musical, the "Big Red Barn." Marly Thomas, a musician, organized a luncheon in his honor, with thirty guests seated at three tables in the residence. Since the weather was temperate, guests mingled in the back garden and Copland sat on the patio wall, with little Frances Thomas in his lap. Marly overheard her tell him that they listened to his music in their car. In the fall of 1976 the Thomases hosted a dinner to welcome seven Egyptians, and the following year again hosted a dinner for five Egyptian visitors and several deans who had traveled to Egypt on an NC State University consulting trip.[34]

LEFT: Guests mingle in the hall and dining room during a Christmas party in 1980. Thomas Family Scrapbook.

RIGHT: During Composer Aaron Copland's guest residency at NC State University in February 1976, he was entertained at the Chancellor's Residence. NCSU Libraries Special Collections Research Center.

ABOVE: At the dedication of the Chancellors Room in the McKimmon Center, in the early 1980s, Dr. Poulton stands with his three predecessors. L to R: Dr. John T. Caldwell, Dr. William Friday (President of the UNC System), Dr. Bruce R. Poulton, Dr. Joab L. Thomas, and Dr. Carey H. Bostian. NCSU Libraries Special Collections Research Center.

on Hillsborough Street. One evening, Frances and Jennifer, ages seven and nine, were standing upstairs looking over the stair railing as a group of students came in. Frances accidently dropped her lollipop on one of the students' heads, which resulted in a big laugh. Mrs. Ruffin kept the Thomas children gently in line, just as she had the Caldwell children.[35]

Chancellor Bruce R. Poulton and Betty Poulton (1982–1989)

Bruce Poulton, an animal scientist trained at Rutgers University, and his wife, Betty, moved into the chancellor's residence from New Hampshire, where he was chancellor of

The Thomases agree that Raleigh was the nicest place they ever lived. Their children thrived during their five years in the Chancellor's Residence. One of Catherine Thomas's high moments was becoming Raleigh's "junior miss" in 1980, when she was a senior at Broughton High School. David Thomas enjoyed his part-time job as a lifeguard at the YMCA pool nearby

the consolidated University System of New Hampshire. His challenge was to raise money to double both faculty salaries and state-of-the-art research space at NC State University. Poulton advocated centers outside the traditional departmental structure, where industry and government leaders sat on a board that set a research agenda for developing new technology, new products, and new public services. He likened it to "uncorking a bottle of ginger ale … suddenly all of this energy bursts loose, in the form of tiny bubbles."[36] In 1984 and 1985, during the last year of Governor Jim Hunt's administration and the first year of Governor Jim Martin's administration, Chancellor Poulton negotiated the transfer of over 800 acres of the farm fields of Dorothea Dix Hospital, south of Western Boulevard and adjacent to NC State University, to the university. A portion of the hospital land, accessed from South Saunders Street and Interstate 40, became the State Farmers Market. During the 1987 NC State University centennial, Poulton and his staff decided to name the new area Centennial Campus, because "it took 100 years to build the main campus and it will take 100 years to build the new campus."[37] The first building on the new campus was the Precision Engineering Research Center, which was first occupied in February 1988. The School of Textiles, the next building, was constructed in 1989. Centennial Campus has become a well-planned "academic city" where private research companies pursue their work in tandem with university faculty, staff, and students.

NC State University became the largest university in the state under Chancellor Poulton. Additions to the campus included the College of Veterinary Medicine, Woods Residence Hall, Fountain Dining Hall, the Administrative Services Building, Jordan Hall for the department of marine, earth, and atmospheric sciences; and a new Pullen Hall for student affairs.[38]

When Bruce and Betty Poulton moved into the Chancellor's Residence, their sons Randall and Jeffrey no longer lived at home, but their two younger children were around much of the time; Cynthia studied law at UNC-Chapel Hill and

BELOW: Bruce Poulton and wife Betty (right) with Dot and I. T. Littleton, Director of Libraries, during the Centennial of 1987. NCSU Libraries Special Collections Research Center.

Peter attended Hargrave Military Academy. In addition to official events at the house, the Poultons often invited smaller groups before or after university basketball games. Chancellor Poulton had a block of seats reserved at Reynolds Coliseum for Friends of the College concerts and often invited his guests to the house before the concerts.

BELOW: Cynthia Poulton's wedding to Arthur Karabelas took place at the Chancellor's Residence in 1984. Poulton Photo Album.

Hattie Ruffin, still the revered housekeeper and cook, came three days a week to care for the residence and to cook. Bruce ate a lot of her fried chicken, which he remembers being delicious even by his Northern standards. She and Betty shared a firm friendship. Soon after moving in, Betty told Hattie that she was going to take the bus downtown to run some errands. Hattie responded heatedly, "You can't take the bus!" Stupefied, Betty asked, "Why not?" Her experience with buses in the Northeast had not prepared her for the South, where public transportation was used almost exclusively by the poor. When the Poultons left the residence in 1989, Mrs. Ruffin retired. She lived in Raleigh until her death in 2008.[39]

Chancellor Larry K. Monteith and Nancy Monteith (1990–1998)

Dr. Larry Monteith, a North Carolina native, NC State University graduate, professor and later dean of the College of Engineering, served as interim chancellor from 1989–1990 and then as chancellor until 1998. One of his primary challenges was the development of Centennial Campus. He believed it had the potential to become a sort of Silicon Valley, which developed in California in the 1940s and 1950s when Stanford University encouraged its faculty and graduates to start their own companies in the area around the campus. In 1969 the Stanford Research Institute (SRI) operated

one of the four original nodes that comprised ARPANET, predecessor of the Internet, and in the 1970s the area was dubbed Silicon Valley.[40] Under Chancellor Monteith's guidance the Centennial Parkway was built and Centennial Campus acquired additional buildings including the first corporate building, the ABB Transmission and Technology Center. In 1996 the Engineering Graduate Research Center (later renamed the Larry K. Monteith Engineering Research Center) opened on Centennial Campus. Dr. Monteith enlarged the library and student center to serve the growing student body. The Visual Arts Center (later the Gregg Museum of Art & Design) was created during his tenure. In 1995 Phi Beta Kappa, the academic honor society allowed at only the highest quality academic institutions in the United States, established a chapter at the university.[41]

When they moved into the chancellor's residence in 1990, Larry and Nancy Monteith brought in a new housekeeper, Doris Atwell, who played a key roll at the residence for fourteen years. Mrs. Atwell had helped the

LEFT: Chancellor's Residence, side view of azaleas and dogwoods in bloom. Poulton Photo Album.

RIGHT: Betty Poulton's Christmas wassail dining room table display. Poulton Photo Album.

LEFT: Former President Jimmy Carter talks with former Governor Jim Hunt at the Chancellor's Residence during an Emerging Issues Forum, 1991. Monteith Family Photo Album.

RIGHT: Larry and Nancy Monteith await their guests at a Christmas reception in the Chancellor's Residence, about 1995. Monteith Family Photo Album.

Monteiths at their previous home and agreed to take on the larger challenge, assuming the new title of house manager. NC State University eventually supplied a second housekeeper, Arlene Crowder, to assist Mrs. Atwell when the number of events grew larger. The Monteiths delighted in hosting breakfasts, lunches, dinners, and parties at the residence with the assistance of Mrs. Atwell and Mrs. Crowder. "We wanted the people on campus to feel that this was their house too, so we had as many events as we could," recalled Larry Monteith.[42] "Even when we weren't hosting an event, we had to keep the house in tip-top shape all the time because people who were alumni or had some other connection to the university would knock

on the door and ask to see the house," added Nancy.[43] Doris and Arlene worked full time Mondays through Fridays. Larry and Nancy hosted Christmas parties for the faculty and staff, with lavish traditional decorations created by Doris and Nancy. Doris also prepared meals for the Monteiths, doing both the shopping and the cooking. Sometimes when the chancellor was away on a trip, Doris spent the night at the house to keep Nancy company. The Monteith children, Carol, Larry, and Steve, were grown, but they visited often—sometimes with their own children in tow.[44]

Chancellor Marye Anne Fox and Jim Whitesell (1998–2004)

For the first time in university history, the woman living in the Chancellor's Residence was the chancellor. A chemistry professor, Marye Anne Fox had degrees from the University of Notre Dame, Cleveland State University, and Dartmouth College. After serving as vice president of research at the University of Texas-Austin, she became NC State University's chancellor in 1998, and led the university in developing nationally known programs in biotechnology,

LEFT: Bill and Doris Atwell, Chancellor's Residence, 1995. Monteith Family Photo Album.

RIGHT: A 1990s Christmas at the Chancellor's Residence. House manager Doris Atwell's traditional Southern apple arrangement over the front door welcomed guests to Larry and Nancy Monteith's holiday party. Monteith Family Photo Album.

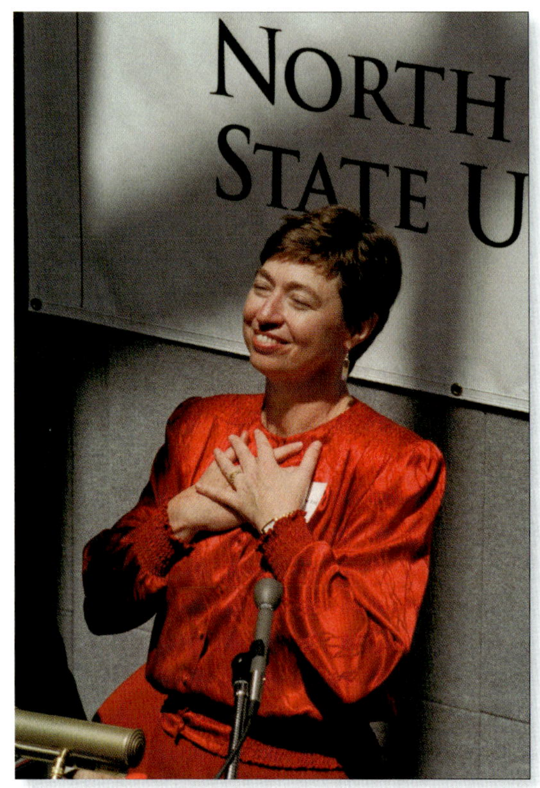

LEFT: Chancellor Marye Anne Fox at a going-away reception, May 2004. Photograph by Roger Winstead, courtesy of NC State University Communications Services.

RIGHT: Jim Whitesell, Marye Ann Fox, and Doris Atwell in the kitchen of the Chancellor's Residence, ca. 2000. Courtesy of Doris Atwell.

nanotechnology, genomics, bioinformatics, and nonwoven textiles. By 2001 the university rose to the rank of sixteenth in the nation in total research expenditures. The number of buildings on Centennial Campus doubled from eight to sixteen, including the Fox Undergraduate Science Teaching Laboratories. The number of industrial partners on Centennial Campus rose from twenty-two in 1999 to seventy-two in 2002. The Ruby McSwain Educational Center at J.C. Raulston Arboretum opened in September 2002. The university's endowment rose from $211 million in 1998 to $312 million by 2002. In 2003 the Department of Biomedical Engineering was established, and the School of Design became a college. The university's research library system, ranked fifty-sixth out of 113 universities in the nation in 1998, rose to the rank of thirty-second by 2004. The Distance Education and Learning Technology Applications (DELTA) was established in 2000 to deliver for-credit courses available online both on campus and off-campus to remote facilities, with more than 600 courses offered by 2004. The RBC Center, where the university men's basketball team plays, was completed. The student body rose to 29,000 (22,000 undergraduates and 7,000 graduate students) by 2004.[45]

Dr. Fox's husband, Jim Whitesell, was a chemistry professor at NC State University, and their four children were grown and living elsewhere. Dr. Fox, a fervent supporter of university athletics, decorated the sunroom/den behind the kitchen, known as the Wolfpack Room, in a red and white theme to celebrate NC State University colors. Jim kept many of his favorite plants in the west wing porch that had been enclosed as a sunroom. Doris Atwell remained as housekeeper for the Foxes until 2004, when Bobbie Cross became the housekeeper. Since Jim Whitesell enjoyed doing the cooking himself, Bobbie worked eight to five Monday through Friday and for special events with responsibilities for housekeeping and security. When the residence hosted dinner parties, she ironed tablecloths and napkins, set the table with the best china and silver, and coordinated with the caterers who supplied the food. The two biggest events of the year were the Christmas open house, when 600 staff and faculty were welcomed into the residence, and the graduation reception for seniors on the lawn, when students stood in line with their parents to have their photos taken with Chancellor Fox.[46]

Chancellor James L. Oblinger and Dr. Diana G. Oblinger (2005–2009)

Dr. James L. Oblinger, a food scientist with degrees in bacteriology and food technology from DePauw University and Iowa State University, came to NC State University from the University of Missouri-Columbia. He served in the university's College of Agriculture and Life Sciences before becoming chancellor in 2005. He continued his predecessors' work in helping the university to deal with the sweeping technical, ethical, and societal changes coming at the world. Enrollment passed 30,000 students during his tenure, and the one billion dollar "Achieve" fund raising campaign for the university was accomplished. Funds were raised to plan the Hunt Library on Centennial Campus, the "library of the future" that would feature a robotic book delivery system, technology-enabled furniture, high-definition video walls, and 3-D computing and visualization spaces when it opened in 2013.

Innovative projects at NC State University developed under Oblinger's leadership include an Outer Banks coastline erosion-control program; a tourism and conservation program on the "Inner Banks" of North Carolina; a family-support system developed by the Department of Social Work in all 100 counties; a joint biomedical engineering program established with UNC-Chapel Hill; and a Virtual Computing Lab created with IBM, Microelectronics Center of North Carolina (MCNC), and other partners to provide virtual access to computing power to run simulations for schools and other institutions. The College of Textiles developed a light-activated fabric that protects medical personnel from deadly viruses and bacteria and first responders from fire damage and chemical exposure. NC State University developed a new technology called "Centia" to convert animal fats, waste grease, and agricultural oils into fuel. The Golden Leaf Biomanufacturing Training and Education

ABOVE: Bobbie Cross, house manager at the Chancellor's Residence, 2004–2011. Photo courtesy of Bobbie Cross.

ABOVE: Chancellor James L. Oblinger and his wife Dr. Diana G. Oblinger in front of the Chancellor's Residence, ca. 2005. Photograph by Roger Winstead, courtesy of NC State University Communications Services.

Center opened on Centennial Campus. The School of Public and International Affairs, which developed ties with China, India, South Korea, Japan and other countries, opened on campus. SAS Hall, built with the support of the Cary-based software company born in the early 1970s out of an NC State University statistics research project, was completed in 2009 for the University's mathematics and statistics program.[47]

When Dr. Oblinger and his wife Diana lived in the chancellor's residence, their grown son Adam visited periodically. The Oblingers redecorated the first floor with new sofas and reupholstered chairs for the living room, new black leather seating and tables for the Wolfpack Room, and new rugs.[48]

Chancellor Randy Woodson and Susan Woodson (2010–)

Randy Woodson, named NC State University's fourteenth chancellor in 2010, is an internationally renowned plant molecular biologist specializing in reproductive processes in agricultural crops. He and his wife Susan grew up in the same small town in Arkansas and became high school sweethearts. He earned his undergraduate degree in horticulture from the University of Arkansas and his M.S. and Ph.D. degrees in plant physiology from Cornell University. Woodson joined the faculty at Purdue University in 1985, then served as department head and dean before accepting the top academic position as provost and executive vice president for academic affairs.

Shortly after his arrival at NC State, he laid out his goals, pledging to recruit and retain star faculty, improve collaboration across disciplines, streamline business operations, and grow the university's endowment. To gain support for this vision of a stronger, leaner NC State, Woodson and his wife, Susan, launched a concerted effort to get to know constituents on campus—and across the globe. In the coming months they would visit dozens of cities in the United States, Europe and Asia, building relationships with thousands of alumni and forging national and international partnerships with leaders in industry, academia, and the public sector.

At home, they kept up an energetic schedule, hosting business leaders, state and local officials, faculty, staff, students, and alumni with gracious hospitality. The university found the Woodsons to be enthusiastic and effective advocates, helping to attract some of the largest private gifts in university history.

In quick order, Woodson launched a series of initiatives, including a first-year student leadership program to promote student success; the Chancellor's Faculty Excellence Program, which aims to attract top faculty in multidisciplinary clusters; the Chancellor's Innovation Fund, which supports promising research; a strategic planning effort to chart NC State's course for the coming decade; and a business realignment effort to improve efficiency in finance and human resources.

Chancellor Woodson, like his predecessors, has continued to oversee the development of Centennial Campus as a national model for university research campuses. It currently houses the colleges of Engineering, Textiles, Veterinary Medicine and the Graduate School along with over sixty companies, government agencies, and non-profits. Major partners located at Centennial Campus include ABB, the U.S. Department of Agriculture, Talecris Biotherapeutics, NOAA National Weather Service, and GlaxoSmithKline. These multidisciplinary research and development complexes let students work with faculty and leaders in their chosen field of study. Hands-on research and academic programs offer real-world experience through internships, corporate shadowing programs, and cooperative education assignments.[49]

Randy and Susan Woodson lived in the Chancellor's Residence while a new official residence was under construction on Centennial Campus, and were joined by their three grown children Samantha, Patrick, and Chloe during holidays and vacations. The Woodsons immediately settled into the house, living "in every corner," recalled Ellen Klingler, events coordinator for the chancellor. "They installed a tv in the sunroom and ate breakfast in there. They hung some of

ABOVE: Chancellor Randy Woodson and Susan Woodson on the front steps of the Chancelloer's Residence. Photograph by Craig McDuffie, 2013.

ABOVE: L to R: Susan Woodson, Dr. Randy Woodson, Gen. Hugh Shelton, L. Worth Harris III, and Ann B. Harris. Chancellor's Residence, March 22, 2011. Gen. Shelton, a North Carolina native and NC State University graduate, had a distinguished Army career in the Special Forces and served as chairman of the Joint Chiefs of Staff from 1997 to 2001. Woodson Family Photo Album.

their own art and brought in art from the Gregg Museum of Art & Design." Susan, an artist, fell in love with the historic character and personality of the restaurants and shops of the Hillsborough Street business district. In 2011 she founded a visual arts cooperative, the Roundabout Art Collective, which opened a gallery across from Chancellor's Residence to promote local art. Later relocated around the corner on Oberlin Road, the collective's gallery of paintings, photographs, glass, silver, pottery, and sculpture by member artists adds an arts dimension to the university neighborhood.

As soon as they moved in, the Woodsons hosted a greatly increased number of events at the old residence, including receptions for new faculty, for student leaders, for university coaches, for North Carolina State University Distinguished Professors, and for faculty members elected to the National Academy of Sciences. One of their first home gatherings was a breakfast for the individuals in the Facilities Department who renovated the residence for their occupancy. In September 2011 they hosted a book signing for *The Man from Mount Gilead*, a biography of Bob Jordan, a university alumnus, state senator and former lieutenant governor. Jordan and his biographer Ned Cline were featured speakers.

Chancellor's Residence, dining room.
Photograph by Craig McDuffie, 2012.

BY SUSAN WOODSON

GEORGIA AND MR. BEASLEY'S ADVENTURES

Was it a shock when I arrived at the residence with my two big, black dogs? These are not small dogs. Georgia is an English shepherd–black lab mix weighing around 75 pounds and Mr. Beasley is a labradoodle weighing around 40 pounds. It would be one thing if my dogs were well-mannered, it is another because they are not. But the staff eventually adjusted to black hair all over the white carpet and holes in the yard from digging, not to mention Mr. Beasley playing in the fountain or Georgia chasing squirrels. A lot of barking and commotion came with the dogs.

Actually the dogs are pretty funny characters and soon began to show their personalities. Several funny stories happened the year we were in the residence. Mr. Beasley is about the friendliest dog you could ever meet. He knows no stranger and would jump in any car if a door was open. One day the UPS man delivered a package and drove off. A minute later I see him coming back. Mr. Beasley had made himself at home in the back of the van. The man had headed out the drive before he noticed him.

There is a gorgeous huge magnolia tree in the front yard of the residence. On a hot day it is a really cool place to rest. We often had homeless people take a break under the tree. They were harmless and it never bothered me. But one day I could not find Mr. Beasley. After searching and calling, I finally looked under the tree and there he was cuddled up with two homeless people taking a nap. I had to go under the tree and excuse myself for disturbing them and pull him out.

Mr. Beasley was quite the wanderer. We had an electric fence to keep the dogs in, but often the collars would be left off and he would make his great escape. I got a call once from the barber shop across Hillsborough Street. They had Mr. Beasley in the shop. I ran over there and he was sitting up in one of the barber chairs as if he was waiting his turn.

Another favorite hangout of Beasley's was the Players Retreat, where he would pick up a French fry or even a burger if he got lucky. I went to pick him up after a call one night and someone was making a leash out of paper napkins. They were going to take him home if no one claimed him. They said they had never seen such a friendly dog.

Georgia isn't my wanderer like Mr. Beasley. She is my hunter. She would sit and watch the squirrels with the hopes of catching one someday. She never did, but she once came up with a baby possum. We were getting ready for a dinner with Governor Hunt. I had let the dogs out one last time before I put them upstairs. As Governor Hunt and his wife Carol were walking up to the front, here comes Georgia with a baby possum in her mouth, which she graciously presented to me on the back steps. Needless to say, I rushed the dogs upstairs and went to get something to move the baby possum which I presumed dead. But as I came back the little possum was scurrying away. I guess possums really do "play dead."

When we were out of town, I often had students stay with the dogs. One night a student came in and saw blood all over the white carpet. Then he noticed a window pane in our back French door had been shattered. Immediately he thought someone had broken in. But before he called the police, he found Georgia huddled in the bathroom bleeding profusely from her paw. He took her to the Vet School and told them they could not let the chancellor's dog die on his watch. It wasn't life-threatening though. A few stitches and Georgia was fine. We figured she had lunged at a squirrel and hit the window pane so hard it shattered. And yes, the blood did come out of the carpet.

Our dogs certainly made themselves at home in the old residence. But since we have moved out to the new residence they have a lot more space to wander. I have had calls from the Alumni Center saying Mr. Beasley was there visiting, or golfers delivering Mr. Beasley home in their golf cart. Georgia doesn't even bother with squirrels anymore when she has so many deer to frolic after. But their favorite destination is going down to the lake and coming home soaked after a nice cool swim in the water.

ABOVE: Randy and Susan Woodson with their dogs, Mr. Beasley and Georgia in the rear garden at the old residence. Photograph by Craig McDuffie, 2013.

Notes

1 Luzette Brown, telephone conversations with the author, September 24 and November 4, 2012.

2 Elizabeth Reid Murray, *Wake, Capital County of North Carolina* (Raleigh, N.C.: Capital County Publishing Company, 1983), vol. 1, 157.

3 Willard B. Gatewood, Jr., *Eugene Clyde Brooks: Educator and Public Servant* (Durham, N.C.: Duke University Press, 1960), vii–viii, 7, 25, 27, 55. All three books were printed by Chicago publishers.

4 United States Census, Wake County, North Carolina, 1930, http://search.ancestrylibrary.com; *Hill's Raleigh City Directory*, 1930 (Richmond, Va.: Hill Directory Co., 1930).

5 United States Census, Wake County, North Carolina, 1930; *Hill's Raleigh City Directory*, 1930; *N. C. S. College of Agriculture and Engineering, Directory of Faculty and Students, 1930–1931* (Raleigh: The College, 1930).

6 *Hill's Raleigh City Directory*, 1930.

7 Downs and Beers, 62; "Live at Home Dinner Menu," Office of the Chancellor Records, UA002.001.001, box 4, folder 16.

8 "Live at Home Dinner Menu."

9 "John W. Harrelson," *Wikipedia*, accessed September 25, 2012, http://en.wikipedia.org/wiki/John_W._Harrelson; Alice Elizabeth Reagan, *NC State University: A Narrative History* (Raleigh: The NC State University Foundation and the NC State University Alumni Association, 1987), 97–106; William S. Powell, *Encyclopedia of North Carolina* (Chapel Hill: University of North Carolina Press, 2006), 832.

10 Downs, "Historical Sketch of NC State University"; "Eugene C. Brooks," *Wikipedia*, accessed September 15, 2012. http://en.wikipedia.org/wiki/Eugene_Brooks.

11 United States Census, Wake County, North Carolina, 1940, http://search.ancestrylibrary.com.

12 Lockmiller, 206-7; Allen, "Hobart Upjohn."

13 Reagan, 112–23; Powell, 832.

14 Lockmiller, 202.

15 John Morris, September 16, 2011 entry, *Goodnight Raleigh* (blog), http://www.goodnightraleigh.com. David Clark, chairman of the college Building Committee at the time, disliked modern architecture. He compared one of the early designs for the union to "cheap and flashy stores at Miami Beach."

16 *Hill's Raleigh City Directory*, 1955 (Richmond, Va.: Hill Directory Co., 1955); Carey Hoyt Bostian interview, "Five Living Chancellors Project [ca. 1975]," Office of the Chancellor Records, UA002.001.008, box 69.

17 Bostian interview.

18 Reagan, 154–64.

19 John T. Caldwell interview, "Five Living Chancellors Project [ca. 1990]," Office of the Chancellor Records, UA002.001.008, box 69.

20 Caldwell interview.

21 Reagan, 184–86, 208; Andy Caldwell, telephone conversation with the author, September 24, 2012.

22 Richard W. Hatch, "Davis Took NCSU Job as Organizational Base," *Raleigh News and Observer*, April 22, 1969.

23 Reagan, 187, 189.

24 Reagan, 189.

25 Reagan, 193, 206; Banks Talley, Jr., telephone interview by the author, November 6, 2012.

26 Andy Caldwell, telephone conversation with the author, September 24, 2012.

27 Lynne Wogan, "Deep South Cooking Is Specialty of House," *Raleigh Times,* October 11, 1972.

28 Alice Caldwell Steele and Andy Caldwell, interview by the author, November 8, 2012; Wogan, "Deep South Cooking Is Specialty of House"; Betsy Marsh, "Chancellor Caldwell's Bride Brings Humor and Enthusiasm to 'Merger,'" *Raleigh News and Observer*, November 10, 1963.

29 Joab Thomas interview, "Five Living Chancellors Project [ca. 1990]," Office of the Chancellor Records, UA002.001.008, box 69.

30 Reagan, 205; Downs, "Historical Sketch of NC State University"; Priscilla Brown, "The Chancellor Speaks: A Look at the Eighties," *NC State University Journal*, February 1980; "Thomas' Praises Sung from N.C. to Alabama," 1981 newspaper clipping, Thomas Family scrapbook. McKimmon Center was named for the director of the Home Demonstration Program in North Carolina from 1911 to 1946.

31 *Raleigh Times* clipping, 1976, Thomas Family Scrapbook.

32 Marly Thomas, telephone interview by the author, November 8, 2012.

33 Judy Bolch, "Entertaining: Many College Heads Frequent Hosts," undated *Raleigh Times* clipping, Thomas Family Scrapbook; Susan Breuer, "Guest Lists Are Long at Chancellor's House," *Raleigh News and Observer*, July 6, 1978.

34 Marly Thomas, email correspondence with the author, January 29, 2013.

35 Marly Thomas telephone interview.

36 Bruce Poulton interview, "Five Living Chancellors Project [ca. 1990]," Office of the Chancellor Records, UA002.001.008, box 69.

37 Ibid.

38 Downs, "Historical Sketch of NC State University."

39 Bruce Poulton, telephone interview by the author, October 29, 2012; interview by the author, November 7, 2012. Bobbie Cross, interview by the author, November 4, 2012.

40 "Silicon Valley," *Wikipedia*, accessed November 16, 2012, http://en.wikipedia.org/wiki/Silicon_Valley.

41 Downs, "Historical Sketch of NC State University"; Larry Monteith interview, "Five Living Chancellors Project [ca. 1990]," Office of the Chancellor Records, UA002.001.008, box 69.

42 Larry and Nancy Monteith, interview by the author, October 4, 2012.

43 Nancy Monteith, telephone conversation with the author, January 11, 2013.

44 Larry and Nancy Monteith interview; Cross interview.

45 Marye Anne Fox, "University Achievements and Growth, 1998–2004," typescript provided by the NC State University Chancellor's Office.

46 Cross interview.

47 James Oblinger, "The State of NC State," September 27, 2007, and "2009 State of NC State University," March 10, 2009, typescripts provided by the NC State University Chancellor's Office.

48 Cross interview.

49 Centennial Campus website, accessed October 30, 2012, http://www.ncsu.edu/about-nc-state/centennial-campus/.

THE POINT AND THE GREGG

A series of five front-gabled red brick pavilions set parallel and connected by hyphens create complex public spaces on the main floor and home spaces on the upper floor. The main floor contains 6,000 square feet with twelve-foot ceilings.

CHAPTER FIVE

The Point and the Gregg Museum of Art & Design

In 2004, university trustees decided to build a new chancellor's residence on the sprawling Centennial Campus rather than to enlarge the old residence to suit the need for entertaining large groups. Such university dwellings have become quasi-public buildings used to promote the university's image. "We don't even like to call it the chancellor's residence because it's really the university's residence," explained Marvin Malecha, dean of the university's College of Design and architect for the new residence.[1] The 9,000-square-foot residence is sited on a spit of land extending into Lake Raleigh, hence the name, "The Point." Michael Harwood, university architect at the time, perceived the residence as a gatehouse for the adjacent old-growth forest that was destined for a housing development but was saved by the campus community's wishes.[2] Knowing how labor-intensive the process of designing the first new chancellor's house in over eighty years would be, Interim Chancellor James Woodward made sure to have the design decisions completed prior to the arrival of Chancellor Randy Woodson in 2010.

Construction materials and artisans from North Carolina were utilized wherever possible so that the project provided maximum benefit to the state's economy. The core design team consisted of Interim Chancellor Woodward; Ann Goodnight, Building Committee chair; Marvin Malecha, design architect; Judy Pickett, interior designer; Ellen Weinstein, associated architect; Kevin MacNaughton, university project manager; Becky K. Bumgardner, university development; contractors John Rufty and Randy Beard of Rufty Homes; and Thomas Skolnicki, university landscape architect, with Derek Blaylock. Genetically-altered, non-warping framing lumber from an NC State University forest—a Weyerhaeuser product developed through the university's DNA research—frames the residence. Locally-made brick that was "tumbled" to give it a vintage patina covers the exterior. This was chosen to match the robust red color of Holladay Hall, the university's original building constructed by state penitentiary prisoners who also fired the bricks. Many people donated their time or reduced their prices because of their love for NC State University. All of the furniture, except for the dining table chairs, was made in North Carolina. (See Appendix for a list of vendors.) Malecha has noted that his design

FACING PAGE: The Point, 1570 Main Campus Drive, Centennial Campus, NC State University, completed in late 2011. Photograph by Dustin Peck, courtesy of the NC State University Chancellor's Office.

BELOW: View of the living room at the Point. Photograph by Dustin Peck, courtesy of the NC State University Chancellor's Office.

FACING PAGE: The Point, interior center hall. Photograph by Dustin Peck, courtesy of the NC State University Chancellor's Office.

BELOW: The Point, Library. Photograph by Dustin Peck, courtesy of the NC State University Chancellor's Office.

inspirations included eighteenth-century colonial buildings along with twentieth-century architects who specialized in residential design, including British architect Sir Edwin Lutyens, Italian architect Carlo Scarpa, American architect Louis Kahn, and contemporary American architect Hugh Newell Jacobsen.

A series of five front-gabled red brick pavilions set parallel and connected by hyphens create complex public spaces on the main floor and home spaces on the upper floor. The main floor contains 6,000 square feet with twelve-foot ceilings. The central pavilion is a broad hall that extends into porches at the front and rear. To the west is a living room and dining room pavilion, then a kitchen and family room pavilion, and finally a service pavilion with a catering kitchen, service area, basement stair, double garage, and elevator. The pavilion east of the central hall contains a library, a grand free-standing staircase, and restrooms. At the extreme east is an attached gazebo.

The largest gathering spaces are the central hall and the kitchen. The hall functions as a welcoming space where up to ninety people can gather around a free-standing staircase that twirls up to the second floor with a balustrade of elegant dark-stained turned balusters arranged in an intriguing pattern. The design team imagined that one day the chancellor, standing on the stair landing that doubles as a podium, would congratulate NC State's first Nobel Prize winner or a coach would welcome a national championship team. The kitchen, large enough to function as an entertainment center of its own, rises to a two-story vaulted ceiling. Its sculptural focus is the large stainless steel range hood that was handmade by a metal fabricator.

The 3,000-square-foot second floor, with nine-foot ceilings, is the private domain of the chancellor and his family. It contains a master suite, three additional bedrooms, kitchenette, sitting room, laundry, and two outdoor porches. An elevator from the basement to the second floor provides a means for family members to enter and exit the residence without interrupting an event.

In late 2011 Chancellor Randy Woodson and his wife Susan moved into The Point. The Woodsons immediately expanded the size and number of events in the residence, possible because of the house's larger size, more efficient floor plan, modern catering facilities, and increased parking capacity. They and their dogs, Georgia and Mr. Beasley, enjoy the beauty of the surrounding grounds and the vista of Lake Raleigh at the rear. The "university's residence" operates as the modern hospitality venue needed for the twenty-first century and adds the warmth of the chancellor's family to the Centennial Campus.

The glass globe on the staircase of the original Chancellor's Residence, its crystal ball, reflects its future as well as its past. The old chancellor's residence on Hillsborough Street will be renovated and expanded. Construction of The Point will allow the Gregg Museum of Art & Design, a jewel hidden in cramped quarters in the Talley Student Center on Cates Avenue, to relocate to the site, and the new Gregg Museum, across Pullen Road from the Memorial Bell Tower, will become a part of the university's gateway. The Gregg's collection of more than 30,000 objects includes major holdings in textiles, clothing, ceramics, folk and Native American art, photography, design, decorative arts, and self-taught art. The museum will be able to present more of its holdings as well as special exhibits in the 15,000-square-foot addition designed by the Freelon Group architects of Durham. Principal Philip Freelon is a 1975 graduate of the university's College of Design.

As we contemplate the Chancellor's Residence, we see how it reflects the past and the personal and administrative lives of the university's leaders for the better part of a century. Ten families have lived there, shared their talent, character, and spirit with the university community, and left their imprint. Eugene and Ida Brooks guided its architectural design and made it their home from 1928 into the early years of the Great

FACING PAGE: The Point, Staircase. Photograph by Dustin Peck, courtesy of the NC State University Chancellor's Office.

LEFT: The Point, view of kitchen. Photograph by Dustin Peck, courtesy of the NC State University Chancellor's Office.

FACING PAGE: The Point, exterior view from rear terrace. Photograph by Dustin Peck, courtesy of the NC State University Chancellor's Office.

BELOW: The Point, Breakfast Room. Photograph by Dustin Peck, courtesy of the NC State University Chancellor's Office.

Depression. John and Elizabeth Harrelson created a haven of hospitality and beauty through the later Depression years, the long years of World War II, and into the university's postwar enrollment boom. It was Elizabeth who erected the formal garden wall, fountain, and terrace at the rear. Carey and Neita Bostian and their three sons filled the residence during the balance of the Fifties. Starting in 1959, John Caldwell, his wife Catherine, and their four children made an even fuller household, necessitating the addition of a den, later known as the Wolfpack Room, behind the kitchen. After Catherine's death, John's second wife Carol Erskine added her two children to the lively mix. Joab and Marly Thomas and their four children moved into the Residence in 1976 and cheerfully interacted with the community for five years. Bruce and Betty Poulton happily resided there for seven years, with regular gatherings before or after sports events or concerts at Reynolds Coliseum. Larry and Nancy Monteith entertained as frequently as possible through most of the 1990s. By the time Marye Anne Fox and her husband Jim Whitesell lived in the house (1998–2004), the west porch had been enclosed as a sunroom, which Jim, a chemistry professor, filled with his favorite plants. James Oblinger and his wife Diana enjoyed the residence from 2005 to 2009. Randy and Susan Woodson, who arrived in 2010, had a short taste of living at the old house before relocating to the new chancellor's residence at the end of 2011.

For eighty-three years the Residence's five bedrooms, upstairs sleeping porch/sunroom, and basement maid's quarters welcomed other family members and guests—elderly parents, nearly grown children home from college, married children with their own children in tow, a succession of housekeepers, and perhaps even a college employee from time to time. Miss Steph Snipes lodged in the basement bedroom during the Brooks's era. Likely the Harrelsons and Bostians had a live-in housekeeper as well. Hattie Ruffin maintained the house and prepared many of the meals for the Caldwells, the Thomases, and the Poultons, although she went home to her own house in the evenings. Doris Atwell kept the residence going under the Monteiths and the Foxes, and Bobbie Cross did the same for the Woodsons. After the 1950s, housekeepers used the maid's room for occasional overnight lodging, and finally the room became the house manager's office.

The house's inhabitants made good use of the spacious grounds, carefully tended by generations of university groundskeepers. Photographs of the house taken by each family fall into two categories: views of the banks of azaleas and drifts of dogwood trees in the springtime and of the front door, stair hall, dining room, and Christmas tree during the holiday season. The huge front oaks held tree swings when children were in the residence, the garden sometimes had summer tomato plants, and, in nice weather, the rear terrace always hosted parties. Graduation receptions took place on the front lawn. During the tumultuous Sixties students massed out front to picket for Civil Rights and other causes. Four-legged creatures have romped about the house and grounds. Chancellor Caldwell holds his dog Shirene in a 1960s family portrait, and Georgia and Mr. Beasley provided enthusiastic welcomes when the Woodsons lived in the Residence.

In the later decades a hedge grew thick and tall along Hillsborough Street, concealing the Residence from view and from the consciousness of passersby. Recently, in anticipation of its new life as the Gregg Museum of Art & Design, gardeners have clipped through the hedge to allow all to enjoy this dignified residential landmark.

Notes

1 Jay Price, "NCSU Shaves Size, Cost of Plan for New House," *Raleigh News and Observer*, February 6, 2010.

2 Michael Harwood, interview by the author, November 9, 2012.

THE RESIDENCE IN PHOTOS

The residence was designed with dual facades to meet its public and private purposes, Janus-like with its public front face to the world and its private rear face towards the woods of Pullen Park.

FACING PAGE: Chancellor's Residence, bedroom No. 3, left front. Photograph by Craig McDuffie, 2012. ABOVE: Front view of the Chancellor's Residence. Photograph by Craig McDuffie, 2012.

ABOVE: Chancellor's Residence, view of front entrance. Photograph by Craig McDuffie, 2012.

ABOVE: Chancellor's Residence, springtime, front view. Photograph by Craig McDuffie, 2012.

ABOVE: Chancellor's Residence hall, looking toward the front door. The persistent belief that the house originally faced south, toward Pullen Park, may reflect the duality of its private and public personality. Architect Hobart Upjohn deliberately faced the house toward Hillsborough Street, giving it an unobtrusive front entrance, whereas the rear entrance facing the park is large and open. Photograph by Craig McDuffie, 2012.

ABOVE: Chancellor's Residence, front view. Photograph by Craig McDuffie, 2012.

ABOVE: Mr. Beasley enjoys the Chancellor's Residence hall. Photograph by Craig McDuffie, 2012.

ABOVE: The graceful curves of the staircase looking down to the front hall. Photograph by Craig McDuffie, 2012.

ABOVE: Den powder room (downstairs). Photograph by Craig McDuffie, 2012.

ABOVE: A silver tea service on the dining room buffet. Photograph by Craig McDuffie, 2012.

ABOVE: Vases of tulips and hydrangeas on the dining table of the Chancellor's Residence. Photograph by Craig McDuffie, 2012.

ABOVE: The living room of the Chancellor's Residence during the Woodson family's brief occupancy. Photograph by Craig McDuffie, 2012.

ABOVE: Chancellor's Residence study. A door to the breakfast room originally stood where the bookcase to the left of the fireplace is now. Photograph by Craig McDuffie, 2012.

ABOVE: The spacious west wing porch of the Chancellor's Residence, enclosed in the late 1900s as a sunroom. Photograph by Craig McDuffie, 2012.

ABOVE: The Caldwell family had this sunroom/den added behind the kitchen in the early 1960s as a playroom for their children. In later years it was called the "Wolfpack Room." Photograph by Craig McDuffie, 2012.

ABOVE: Upstairs hall landing. Photograph by Craig McDuffie, 2012.

ABOVE: Chair in left front bedroom No. 3. Photograph by Craig McDuffie, 2012.

ABOVE: View of the bedrooms west of the stair landing. Photograph by Craig McDuffie, 2012.

ABOVE: Chancellor's Residence, bedroom No. 2, right rear. This served as the original master bedroom. Photograph by Craig McDuffie, 2012.

ABOVE: Chancellor's Residence, bedroom No. 1, left rear. Photograph by Craig McDuffie, 2012.

ABOVE: Chancellor's Residence, bedroom No. 3, left front. Photograph by Craig McDuffie, 2012.

ABOVE: Chancellor's Residence, bedroom No. 5, east wing bedroom. Photograph by Craig McDuffie, 2012.

ABOVE: Rear garden of the Chancellor's Residence. Photograph by Craig McDuffie, 2012.

ABOVE: Rear garden swing. Photograph by Craig McDuffie, 2012.

ABOVE: The west terrace, adjoining the west wing sunroom, hosted many parties in nice weather. Photograph by Craig McDuffie, 2012.

APPENDIX

The Point, 1570 Main Campus Drive, Centennial Campus, Raleigh, North Carolina

APPENDIX

The Point, NC State University Chancellor's Residence

1570 Main Campus Drive, Centennial Campus. List of subcontractors and suppliers:

- *Appliances:* Bill Stuart, Fergusons Enterprises
- *Cabinets:* Jimmy Thompson, Thompsons Cabinet Shop
- *Cabinet and Door Hardware:* Rick Jacobs, Taps & Latches
- *Countertops:* Laura Grandlienard, Rockin'teriors
- *Driveway:* Tri-City Contractors, concrete; European Expressions, stone
- *Drywall finish:* Steve Roof, Professional Drywall Solutions
- *Electrical:* Donnie Cunningham, O'Patricks Electrical Contractors
- *Elevator:* Tommy Faulkner, REAL Elevator Solution, Inc.
- *Gas Fireplaces:* Chris O'Brien, Fireside Hearth and Home
- *Garage Doors:* Katie Dickinson, Lighthouse Garage Doors
- *Gutters:* Jon Cagle, Trademark Seamless Gutters
- *Hardwood floors:* John McCullough, DownUnder Flooring
- *Heating & Air Conditioning:* Tom Paonessa, Warren Hay Mechanical
- *Home Automation:* Jon Walton, Carolina Custom Sound & Security
- *Interior trim:* Mike Andrews, Tri-City Interiors
- *Insulation:* Myers Professional Insulation
- *Iron rails:* Chris Longski, Dakota Fab & Welding
- *Light Fixtures (decorative):* Design Lines; Butler Electrical Supply of High Point
- *Marble/Tile:* Paul Cacciato, European Expressions
- *Paint:* exterior and interior: Sharon Stein, Stein Finishes
- *Plumber:* Steve Dixon, Alliance Plumbing
- *Plumbing Fixtures:* Rick Jacobs, Taps & Latches
- *Roofing:* John Cagle, Trademark Roofing Company
- *Shower doors:* Mike Wilkins, Carolina Glass & Mirror
- *Surveyor:* Withers & Ravenel
- *Surround Sound/Media:* Jon Walton, Carolina Custom Sound & Security
- *Termite Certification:* Smith Exterminating

BIBLIOGRAPHY

Valuable information about the Chancellor's Residence and its history

Bibliography

The following individuals provided the author with valuable information about the Chancellor's Residence and its history:

- Bishir, Catherine, interviews, January 10 and 30, 2013.
- Brown, Luzette, telephone conversations, September 24 and November 4, 2012.
- Caldwell, Andy, interview, November 8, 2012; telephone conversation, September 24, 2012.
- Cross, Bobbie, interview, November 4, 2012.
- Harwood, Michael, interview, November 9, 2012.
- Michael, Michelle, email correspondence, October 15, 2012.
- Monteith, Larry, interview, October 4, 2012.
- Monteith, Nancy, interview, October 4, 2012; telephone conversation, January 11, 2013.
- Poulton, Bruce, telephone interview, October 29, 2012; interview, November 7, 2012.
- Steele, Alice Caldwell, interview, November 8, 2012.
- Talley, Banks, Jr., telephone interview, November 6, 2012.
- Thomas, Marly, telephone interview, November 8, 2012; email correspondence Janurary 29, 2013.

In addition, transcripts of interviews with Chancellors Bostian, Caldwell, Thomas, Poulton, and Monteith can be found in the NCSU Libraries Special Collections Research Center:

- Five Living Chancellors Project. Office of the Chancellor, Marye Anne Fox Records, UA 002.001.008, box 69. Special Collections Research Center, NCSU Libraries, NC State University.
- The NCSU Libraries Special Collections was the major source of information for this project. Specific citations to this collection can be found in the notes.
- Office of the Chancellor Records. Special Collections Research Center, NCSU Libraries, NC State University.

Other Sources:

- *Alumni News (North Carolina State College)* See the notes for citations to issues published in February 1923; January, May, and October 1924; October 1925; and November 1927.
- Bishir, Catherine W., Charlotte V. Brown, Carl R. Lounsbury, and Ernest H. Wood III. *Architects and Builders in North Carolina: A History of the Practice of Building*. Chapel Hill: University of North Carolina Press, 1990. In particular, see "The Professionalization of Building, 1900–1945" by Charlotte V. Brown and "Architects and Builders Since 1945" by Ernest H. Wood III.
- Bishir, Catherine W., and Michael T. Southern. *A Guide to the Historic Architecture of Piedmont North Carolina*. Chapel Hill: University of North Carolina Press, 2003.
- Brown, Priscilla. "The Chancellor Speaks: A Look at the Eighties." *NC State University Journal*, February 1980.
- Centennial Campus website, http://www.ncsu.edu/about-nc-state/centennial-campus/.

- Clark, Roger H. *School of Design: The Kamphoefner Years 1948–1973*. Raleigh: NC State University College of Design Publications, 2007.
- De Miranda, Cynthia. "Historic Architectural Resources Survey Report, TIP No. U-4447." Hillsborough Street Improvement Project #1. Raleigh: N.C.: Historic Preservation Office, 2004.
- Downs, Murray Scott. "Historical Sketch of NC State University." Historical State website, http://historicalstate.lib.ncsu.edu/histories/historical-sketch-of-north-carolina-state-university.
- Downs, Murray Scott, and Burton F. Beers. *NC State University: A Pictorial History*. Raleigh: NC State University Alumni Association, 1986.
- Fletcher, Bannister. *A History of Architecture on the Comparative Method*. 16th ed. New York: Charles Scribner's Sons, 1956.
- Fox, Marye Anne. "University Achievements and Growth, 1998–2004" (typescript provided by the NCSU Chancellor's Office).
- Gatewood, Willard B., Jr. *Eugene Clyde Brooks: Educator and Public Servant*. Durham, N.C.: Duke University Press, 1960.
- *Goodnight Raleigh Blog*, blog entry by John Morris, September 16, 2011.
- *Hill's Raleigh City Directory*. 1930 (Richmond, Va.: Hill Directory Co., 1930). 1955 (Richmond, Va.: Hill Directory Co., 1955).
- Little, M. Ruth. "Longview Gardens Historic District." National Register Nomination. Raleigh: N.C. Historic Preservation Office, 2009.
- Little, M. Ruth. *The Town and Gown Architecture of Chapel Hill, North Carolina, 1795–1975*. Chapel Hill: The Preservation Society of Chapel Hill, 2006.
- Lockmiller, David A. *History of the North Carolina State College of Agriculture and Engineering of the University of North Carolina, 1889–1939*. Raleigh: The General Alumni Association of the North Carolina State College of Agriculture and Engineering, 1939.
- Martin, Jennifer, Sarah Woodard, Clay Griffith, and Cynthia de Miranda. "Maiden Lane Historic District." National Register Nomination. Raleigh: N. C. Historic Preservation Office, 2005.
- Morris, John. January 10, June 29, and September 16, 2011 entries. *Goodnight Raleigh* (blog). http://www.goodnightraleigh.com.
- Murray, Elizabeth Reid. *Wake, Capital County of North Carolina*. Raleigh: Capital County Publishing Company, 1983.
- *N. C. S. College of Agriculture and Engineering, Directory of Faculty and Students, 1930–1931*. Raleigh: The College, 1930.
- Nichols, Keith, Dave Pond, and Matthew Robbins. "History of the Chancellor's Residence." *This Red House* (blog). http://web.ncsu.edu/this-red-house/history.
- *North Carolina Architects & Builders: A Biographical Dictionary*. Raleigh: NCSU Libraries Digital Scholarship & Publishing Center, 2009–. http://ncarchitects.lib.ncsu.edu. Entries for Charles W. Barrett, Charles L. Carson, C.C. Hook, Charles Barton Keen, H.P.S. Keller, Frank B. Simpson, and Hobart Upjohn.
- James Oblinger. "The State of NC State," September 27, 2007, and "2009 State of NC State University," March 10, 2009 (typescripts provided by the NC State University Chancellor's Office).
- Powell, William S. *Encyclopedia of North Carolina*. Chapel Hill: University of North Carolina Press, 2006.
- "Pullen Park History." City of Raleigh website, accessed October 4, 2012. http://www.raleighnc.gov/arts/content/PRecRecreation/Articles/PullenParkHistory.html.

- "R. Stanhope Pullen" (Marker H-91). North Carolina Highway Historical Marker Program website. Raleigh: North Carolina Department of Cultural Resources. http://www.ncmarkers.com.
- *Raleigh News and Observer.* See the notes for citations to undated clippings and to issues published in May 15 and October 13, 1927; November 10, 1963; April 22, 1969; July 6, 1978; and February 6, 2010.
- *Raleigh Times*. See the notes for citations to undated clippings and to the issue published on October 11, 1972.
- Reagan, Alice Elizabeth. *NC State University: A Narrative History*. Raleigh: The NC State University Foundation and the NC State University Alumni Association, 1987.
- Schumann, Marguerite E. *Strolling at State: A Walking Guide to NC State University*. Raleigh: NC State University Alumni Association and NC State University Foundation, 1973.
- United States Census, Wake County, North Carolina, 1930 and 1940. http://search.ancestrylibrary.com.
- *Wikipedia*. http://en.wikipedia.org/wiki/. Entries for Eugene C. Brooks, John W. Harrelson, Warren H. Manning, Hugh Shelton, and Silicon Valley.

RIGHT: Upstairs landing. Photograph by Craig McDuffie, 2012.

INDEX

Index

Photographic Index

The majority of historical photographs were provided by the NCSU Libraries Special Collections Research Center. The following photographers contributed to this volume.